BFI Film Classics

The BFI Film Classics is a series of books that introduces, interprets and celebrates landmarks of world cinema. Each volume offers an argument for the film's 'classic' status, together with discussion of its production and reception history, its place within a genre or national cinema, an account of its technical and aesthetic importance, and in many cases, the author's personal response to the film.

For a full list of titles available in the series, please visit our website: www.palgrave.com/bfi

'Magnificently concentrated examples of flowing freeform critical poetry.'
Uncut

'A formidable body of work collectively generating some fascinating insights into the evolution of cinema.'
Times Higher Education Supplement

'The series is a landmark in the history of film criticism.'
Quarterly Review of Film and Video

Editorial Advisory Board

Geoff Andrew, British Film Institute
Edward Buscombe, University of Sunderland
Lalitha Gopalan, University of Texas at Austin
Lee Grieveson, University College London
Nick James, Editor, Sight & Sound

Laura Mulvey, Birkbeck College, University of London
Dana Polan, New York University
B. Ruby Rich, University of California, Santa Cruz
Amy Villarejo, Cornell University
Zhen Zhang, New York University

8½

[Otto e mezzo]

D. A. Miller

A BFI book published by Palgrave Macmillan

© D. A. Miller 2008

First published in 2008 by
PALGRAVE MACMILLAN
Houndmills, Basingstoke, Hampshire RG21 6XS and
175 Fifth Avenue, New York, N.Y. 10010
Companies and Representatives throughout the world

on behalf of the

BRITISH FILM INSTITUTE
21 Stephen Street, London W1T 1LN
www.bfi.org.uk

There's more to discover about film and television through the BFI.
Our world-renowned archive, cinemas, festivals, films, publications and learning resources are
here to inspire you.

PALGRAVE MACMILLAN is the global academic imprint of the Palgrave Macmillan division of
St. Martin's Press, LLC and of Palgrave Macmillan Ltd. Macmillan® is a registered trademark in
the United States, United Kingdom and other countries.
Palgrave is a registered trademark in the European Union and other countries.

All rights reserved. No reproduction, copy or transmission of this publication may be made
without written permission. No paragraph of this publication may be reproduced, copied or
transmitted save with written permission or in accordance with the provisions of the Copyright,
Designs and Patents Act 1988, or under the terms of any licence permitting limited copying
issued by the Copyright Licensing Agency, 90 Tottenham Court Road, London W1T 4LP.
Any person who does any unauthorised act in relation to this publication may be liable to
criminal prosecution and civil claims for damages.

The author(s) have/has asserted his/her/their right(s) to be identified as the author(s) of this work
in accordance with the Copyright, Designs and Patents Act 1988.

Series cover design: Ashley Western
Series text design: ketchup/SE14

Set by D R Bungay Associates, Burghfield, Berkshire
Printed in China

This book is printed on paper suitable for recycling and made from fully managed and sustained
forest sources. Logging, pulping and manufacturing processes are expected to conform to the
environmental regulations of the country of origin.

British Library Cataloguing-in-Publication Data
A catalogue record for this book is available from the British Library

ISBN 978-1-84457-231-1

Contents

Prologue

EIGHTY AND A HALF. It was bound to happen that Federico Fellini's *8½*, which even hostile critics praised for its inventiveness when it came out in 1963, would follow its hero into the diminished condition of middle age, where, as one of those critics insisted at the time, it 'doesn't matter a damn'. *8½* is now somewhere between forty and death – ageless only in the self-deceived sense that we reserve for the great beauties of our youth, that is, for our youth itself. Its datedness is not the usual case of yesterday's breakthrough becoming today's convention (though it is almost inconceivable to us now that *8½*'s memory sequences once had to be sepia-tinted for comprehension in the Italian provinces). On the contrary, so little stiffness shows in the film's joints that only a few years ago R.E.M. copied the opening traffic jam for a music video. Even loosely mimicked, and voided of Fellini's allegory of midlife impasse, the sequence held its own against the latest in visual stimulation. And thanks to the labours of Mediaset in Italy and Criterion in the US, the spots, lines and lesions that gradually disfigured the circulating prints have been almost unnaturally washed and buffed away in new negatives and DVD editions, so that Fellini's images are eerily pristine: the film now looks as it might have done before anybody saw it.

No, *8½* is not suffering from material disrepair or even from a strictly formal kind of decrepitude; it is suffering merely from *cultural aging*, from the simple fact that it lives on, just as it was, while the surrounding conditions that helped make it a 'moment' in cinema history erode, disappear or change beyond recognition. With the ebbing of this moment, the film must put up with a series of minor but ominous indignities – or so they seem to anyone who knew *8½* at an earlier age. Its ratings in polls of 'the greatest films of all time' have begun to drop. Intellectuals desert it, with the distaste of epicures for a staple.[1] Meanwhile, those stewards of the future, the young, watch the R.E.M. video innocent of any suspicion of *hommage*; if anything, they might recall Joel Schumacher's *Falling Down* (1993), which replicates the same sequence, turning it into an occasion for road rage. How should they recognize *8½* when art houses have become as scant as the art films once regularly shown in them? Mass culture, grown more overbearing than any elite culture ever was, makes the very project of an art film, with its unapologetic embrace of art's self-estrangement, look pretentious and quaint, like wearing a beret.

Nor is it really a correction of this point to observe that, among mass culture's advance guard, many know perfectly well where that music video came from, and their number is on the rise. This only means that 'art house' is now too feeble to resist the gathering steam of its pop hijacking, a misrecognition that seems as bad as no recognition at all. Just as designer labels have come to adorn even our humblest jeans, so the *fantasy* of an art film now embellishes every movie that rolls off the production line. The bigger the Hollywood release, the more likely it is to boast an 'auteur' who would turn its mandatory ideological clichés into so many intriguingly hidden figures in the carpet. We are asked to give Gore Verbinski's development the same degree of attention we formerly accorded Mizoguchi's. Working against the mass-culture industry – often while also working within it – auteurs were necessarily scarce. Now that one has become indispensable to every film's marketing, they are a dime a dozen.

All this is to say that even *8½*'s restored freshness seems a bit of a mockery, all the more cruel because we aren't allowed to notice, much less complain about, the ethos that is missing. It is not altogether heartening that mass-produced cocktail napkins make cleaner examples of modernist aesthetic purity than the now cracked and discoloured Mondrian canvases that are the source of their patterns. The very brightness of the new *8½* improves our view of a contemporary landscape where the achievement of the old one is no longer possible, no longer even desirable.

This cultural obsolescence is not an endless process; it will last only so long as 8½ remains in what is called 'living memory': so long as there survives the generation whom it first took by surprise. When the last member of that first audience has disappeared, the giant tree may or may not fall in the forest; there will be no one left either to hear its distinctive thud or to marvel that, after all, it is still standing. 8½ will belong wholly to the archives, where, though it might live forever, it will certainly be dead. The present phase before extinction, therefore, strikes me as a uniquely propitious time for writing about the film. This darkling maturity will no more recur than the blissful dawn enjoyed by early birds: one is only young once, but one is only middle-aged once, too. Admittedly, any writing that truly seized the late hour would be anxious ('what is left to say?'), sentimental ('who cares to hear it?'), self-indulgent ('but I will proceed nonetheless'); and its author, himself perforce middle-aged, would be certain to confuse the film with the course of his own life. But there, precisely, would lie the point of the exercise: that someone would lend himself, *while anyone still could*, to dramatising the film's own perverse willingness – likewise anxious, sentimental and self-indulgent – to inhabit a state of dubious social pertinence. After all, no film dwells on – or could be said to dwell *in* – the sense of futility latent in cultural production more than 8½. Its director hero is the first to admit that he has 'nothing to say', and despite that admission persists in the resolve 'to say it anyway'. The cultural death sentence currently impending over 8½ was passed long ago by the film's own theme, and more than duly recorded by its extravagant style. Outdatedness is but a late historical manifestation of the untimeliness that the film affirms for itself – as defiantly as if it were baring a shameful brand, and as lightly as if this brand were the gladdest tidings. It may be a good thing to restore a film to its cultural context, to put it back in the old-fashioned frame from which it succeeded in popping out. But there is a better thing to do for 8½, and that is to restore the film to what never was in fashion, and never could have been: its irrelevance.

1 From No One to Someone

GA/FF/DA. The great conceit to which *8½* is considered to owe its place in cinema history only starts with the fact that the hero is a film director. Guido Anselmi (Marcello Mastroianni), the hero in question (hereafter GA), is at once much more than a director, and much less. On the one hand, he is an auteur, a director who is also the artistic originator of his films, and enjoys international celebrity as such. On the other hand, floundering in full-blown midlife crisis, he shirks even the basic tasks of his métier to the point where he hardly knows what film he is supposed to be making. No longer the master he had shown himself in previous works, he has suddenly, inexplicably become embarrassed by the demands of authorship and reluctant to assume anything about it – except, that is, its central position, which is the one thing that he seems not to run away from. Only at the end of *8½*, literally at the last minute, does he discover his subject, which proves to be none other than this struggle to find it. 'All this confusion is me, myself.' The insight allows him to resume his megaphone and, while Federico Fellini's film is ending, GA's finally begins.

As even this bald summary suggests, GA cannot simply represent 'a' director (such as we might find, less centrally positioned, in Vincente Minnelli's *The Bad and the Beautiful* [1952]); he incarnates 'the' director, the one responsible for the film we are watching. This film insinuates a mirror-construction in which we're to understand GA as an image of FF, and GA's story as a reflection of – and on – the coming-to-be of *8½* itself.[2] Originally entitled 'La bella confusione' ('A Fine Confusion'), *8½* repeatedly breaches the normally airtight levels of author and character, story-telling and story told. More than once, GA astonishes us by whistling a tune we have just heard on the soundtrack or by appearing in a shot that began as his own point of view. Such Escher effects only make sense under the assumption that GA's project and FF's achievement, if never identical, are always concomitant; at every moment, each is critically present to the other, and neither can be understood outside this 'confusing' mutual cross-referencing.

The insignia of this concomitance is the title itself, *8½*. The single line of an '8', of course, already contains two circles. But the film's famous logo – the first image we see on screen – takes the doubling further: the black ovals inside these circles have been pinched so that each half of the '8' silhouettes a miniature of the

whole. The figure suggests, too, the Möbius strip, whose confounding continuity of inside and outside is conventionally represented as a three-dimensionalised '8' – see Escher's drawings or, even more to the point, the inspired poster for *8½*'s first release in the Soviet Union. As for the fraction, it literalises the ambiguity between one and two inherent in the '8' – and in the process renders the title a number midway between two integers, two 'whole' units. '8½' thus heralds the monstrous hybrid, existential and conceptual, that no analysis of the film can avoid: GA/FF.[3]

No analyst can avoid it either. It is impossible to watch this film without entering the mirror-maze and being refashioned therein as a reflection of the hero/author.

The objection made to *8½* at the time of its release – that the hero's problems couldn't possibly interest any viewer who wasn't a film director – never made sense except as a defence mechanism against the fact that the film seduces *every* viewer into the fantasy of authorship, of doubling GA/FF both psychically and creatively. I am not sure that, as a critic, one can resist this grandiosity; the put-upon tone of those who try only confirms how far they have fallen victim to an imposition. I prefer to accept the absurd identification, to take myself – howsoever I can – for 'the very person' meant to be writing about *8½*.

AUTHOR! AUTHOR! In the auteurist atmosphere that suffused European cinema in the late 1950s, Fellini's invention was waiting to be discovered. The intellectual premise of auteurism was disarmingly simple: a work of art demanded an artist, and in the case of film, this could only be the film director, who controlled its structure and meaning much like the 'author' of a novel or poem. But its effect was to launch an unprecedented promotion of the director in film culture, to such an extent that his charismatic name – Bergman! Antonioni! Godard! – became as crucial to selling the art film as the glamorous image of the star continued to be in Hollywood advertising. Within a couple of years after *Cahiers du cinéma* espoused 'the politics of the auteur', the auteur throned over film journals, film festivals and art house marquees alike, until he virtually became a synonym for the art film itself, now conceived as a *cinéma d'auteurs*. (*8½* came out at a high-water mark in this cinema's expansion: in New York City, a key outpost of its empire, the film did not simply open *at* an art house; it opened, as the inaugural attraction, the house itself. This was the Festival Theatre, built and operated by Joseph E. Levine, then Fellini's US distributor; its prime location, just off Fifth Avenue at 6 West 57th Street, has since been converted to retail.)

Like any other imperialism, that of the auteur implied a logic of 'the next step'. On such a horizon, Fellini's conceit was eminently thinkable. If (as auteurist critics liked to insist) the auteur was the

A SALUTE...FROM THE MOTION PICTURE INDUSTRY...
TO NEW YORK'S NEWEST SHOWCASE

THE
FESTIVAL
THEATRE

real subject of his films, then why shouldn't he become the *ostensible* subject as well? With everyone in the audience clamouring 'Author! Author!', why not acknowledge, why not oblige the demand by stepping out from behind the curtains? And not briefly, à la Hitchcock, or in a subordinate role, à la Godard in *Le Mépris* (*Contempt*, 1963), but in the full strength of his centrality? With 8½, the auteur, whom cinephile culture had been featuring everywhere but in the feature, now made a spectacle of *himself*. The effect was galvanising; to many intellectuals, it seemed as if, with this self-reflection, cinema had finally realised its theoretical 'concept'. Directors in particular saw in 8½ the emancipation proclamation of 'personal' film-making, and could hardly wait to celebrate their freedom by producing, one after another, slavish imitations of Fellini's film.

ZÉRO DE CONDUITE. But it is not simply the impetus of a triumphant auteurism that speaks in 8½'s governing conceit. As Fellini well knew, this conceit could only be undertaken as a piece of deliberate rule-breaking. Crucial to the auteur's divinity had been an obliquity, even an abstraction of his person, that auteurist critics took good care to reinforce. They were looking for the (thematic, stylistic) consistency of a director's signature, not for the details of his life or the specifics of his social condition. Though André Bazin famously complained that the 'politics of the auteur' risked becoming 'an aesthetic cult of personality', this cult was no more interested in the actual biography of Renoir or Rossellini than its political counterpart was willing to tell the masses everything that they were afraid to ask about Stalin or Mao. Hitchcock's cameos are exceptions meant to prove this rule of good authorship. In a landscape populated by stars, the heavy, homely Hitchcock comes on screen only to establish his unsuitability to a fiction where his person is laughable, even a bit monstrous. For that reason, the incarnation is swiftly aborted; and the man who is too much disappears into the auteur who is everything.

Obviously, many an auteur had put himself into his work before 8½, but two precautions had always kept the autobiographical subtext from becoming the bad form that 8½ – where Fellini cast the part of GA's mistress with his own – was widely felt to display. One was structural: the difference in narrative status that separates author and character and that requires any intimacy between them to take place indirectly, across great ontological barriers. This difference is particularly pronounced in film, whose grammar (certain marginal experiments aside) lacks the first person; even when a voiceover says 'I', the camera inclines to show us a 'he' or a 'she'. The other precaution was rhetorical: a certain mist of tact, of understatement, enveloped the autobiographical aspect of a film so that it never interfered with – it could only enhance – a universal understanding of the story. The personal merely went to show that there was nothing very personal about it, nothing, at any rate, that couldn't be absorbed into a person's general social representativeness.

In this respect, Visconti's *Il gattopardo* (*The Leopard*) and Godard's *Le Mépris*, each of which came out in the same year as 8½, are both better-behaved auteurist productions. In *Il gattopardo*, the film's aristocratic director, Count Don Luchino, no doubt draws some part of his likeness in the film's aristocratic hero, Prince Don Fabrizio, but given the film's mid-nineteenth-century setting, there can be no resemblance in point of film-making. Conversely, in *Le Mépris*, Godard employs the metacinematic device of the film-within-a-film, but he sets this self-reflection at an off angle to his central story. And it is difficult to think of the fictive director, called 'Fritz Lang', as an authorial surrogate for Godard, since the former is played by Fritz Lang himself, with the latter in the role of his assistant. If the biographical Godard is at all referenced in this distancing structure, it is only as a *rat de cinémathèque*, a lowly life-form over whom, from his place in the auteurist pantheon, Lang towers like a god.

In breaking auteurism's cardinal rule of personal discretion, Fellini's conceit was felt to be just that: the arrogance of a deplorable first flowering in the culture of narcissism. The vehemence with which his so-called self-indulgence was denounced can hardly be overstated, with many critics believing themselves under civic obligation to flaunt their disgust. 'It wallows in self-abuse,' wrote Joseph Bennett of the film, linking it to public masturbation and rolling in shit. Pauline Kael, in her review, compared Fellini first to a vain bisexual actor and then, lest the innuendo be thought obscure, to an hysterical couturier. All this, and more, in the name of good manners.[4]

THESIS. In 1963, then, there were two kinds of people in the world regarding Fellini's fictional incarnation. For the enthusiasts, the trope of author-as-person had realised the manifest destiny of auteurism to take pride of place in front of the camera as well as behind it; it pioneered a species of film-making that was intellectually reflexive and personally intimate at once. For the detractors, the same trope had allowed Fellini to follow, all too precipitously, the course of least artistic resistance; for what could be easier, or more facile, than self-indulgence? But both parties agreed on what they were seeing: an affirmation of author and person alike, each enhancing the other's value. Whether you cheered or contested the affirmation, you didn't doubt that it was one.

That was how *8½* looked, not only in 1963, but also all through its youth.

Now, in the film's middle age – or so it seems to me – the evidence is increasingly visible that Fellini's ground-breaking conceit is not the confident or crass self-manifestation we once supposed. Now, on the contrary, it is apparent that the conceit is being constantly pulled back by a massive unwillingness *to go through with it*. Though he spearheads auteurist expansion, this auteur is also prey to strange fits of compunction when it comes to actually occupying the newly conquered territory; and again and again his cocky exhibitionism proves sapped by a meek and reclusive shame. In short, the trope of author-as-person betrays a mutual insufficiency, a common unsureness, in author *and* person. Let me call this conflict in the film – between affirming and retracting its ruling conceit – the author-person's *reluctance* (from Latin *reluctari*, to struggle or resist). The reasons for it lie at the core of what *8½* is still asking us to understand.

TRAFFIC JAM. Fellini's decision to make GA a director like himself was made in panic and desperation. Even in reminiscence, he almost courts Kael's imputation of hysteria:

For two months, I worked on the script with Flaiano and Pinelli, but it wasn't convincing because I couldn't decide on what the protagonist did for a living. … I felt myself floundering; I was on the brink of abandoning the project. But I gave the order to start, that we begin now, because someone or something was going to intervene to force me, to shame me into making this picture. The simple fact that I couldn't face telling my loyal troupe that I was about to abandon a film whose subject I knew nothing about revealed my subject to me: a director who no longer knows what film he wants to make.

I made the picture so that I wouldn't have to be shamed into making it. But 'something or someone' *did* shame Fellini into making *8½*: the very fear of that something or someone. Far from leaving shame behind, he seems to have needed to *shame himself* into making the film ('I couldn't face telling my loyal troupe'). And as we'll see, shaming himself *into* making the film is not so far from shaming himself *in* making the film.

For the reluctance, the 'floundering', behind Fellini's decision to make the protagonist a director like himself does not vanish once that decision has been made. It continues into the actual film, where the hero too is in a panic about his embodiment. Instead of simply taking the auteur's incarnation for granted, 8 ½ begins, like a creation myth, by dramatising a primordial flux in which authorial being is undecided – torn or suspended between various forms it might assume. This obscure, indeterminate being, this protoplasmic ur-Guido, occupies the famous opening sequence. 'He' (only so much seems sure) first appears in mere outline behind the wheel of a car mired in a vast traffic jam. His meagre delineation is scored to a silence – baffling in a bottleneck – that only adds to our sense, as the film is beginning, that it hasn't yet begun *properly*. Suddenly, the congestion is no longer simply outside his vehicle. Toxic fumes proliferate from within, as if the ventilating system had been murderously funnelling the exhaust pipes of all the cars around him. The buttons on the dashboard prove good for nothing and, just when he most needs air, the car doors and windows won't open.

We will soon be invited to call this sequence 'GA's nightmare', a caption that covers rather too well its narrative incoherence. For we can't know that it is a nightmare on first viewing, nor can we know that it belongs to GA or any other 'person'. What orients the sequence is not a *character* – the narrative representation of a person – but a *figure*, the place-holder for a (somehow) missing person. The ambiguity of this figure is twofold: visually, he is never seen directly or fully; and socially, he is never recognisable as someone in particular. Like a figure in cheap fiction, ur-Guido looms and lurks, exempt from that 'tyranny of the particular' (Proust) that governs the traditional presentation of character and defines the 'people' with whom he shares the scene.

Though equally anonymous, these others have exceptionally vivid middle-aged faces lined with that legibility, that social text, which we call, not for nothing, 'character'. Their emphatic, overstated features are the equivalent of the defining mannerisms of so-called flat characters in Austen or Dickens. No story is told of these drivers and passengers, but, as a result of their faces, they already exist in the third person, in conventionally narratable form. After 8½, of course, Fellini

would become famous for his faces. But it is essential to see beyond this early trademarking of the 'Fellini face' to the social condition – the condition of being social – that is critically condensed in it. In star-based cinema, Fellini faces are, as we say, unsightly. Repulsive not just in their lack of youth and beauty, or in the exaggeration of their features, but even more for their thrusting insistence on remaining withal 'in our face' (as though, not having one, we could only have theirs!), these faces are shameful and shameless at once.

They are shameful because, overparticularised, they somehow tell too much about the souls of their owners; the lines on them seem drawn there – as GA will later draw whorish eyebrows over his mistress's eyes – by a ruthless caricaturist. They are shameless, too, because a certain impenitence, even insolence, dominates these faces; they emit the brazen, barbed personality required to go through life wearing them. Yet, whether embarrassing or barefaced, they never change expression; the images might as well be stills, and the people stiffs. It is as if a key aspect of our social existence – our life in the third person – were the submission to just such mortuary paralysis; in the supposedly private teleports of our cars, we sit already posed for photos that could equally appear on a driver's licence or a fatality report.

Ur-Guido lacks the mortifying detail of such faces. As befits his status as figure, he is shot from the back; his body is revealed only in fragments, or in billowing, merely suggestive silhouette. And though he is aggressively stared at, it is unclear that he is *seen*, or if he is, *how* he is seen. The lack of a reverse shot here – at whom are those faces staring? – does not, then, empower the figure. The meaning of this lack is not that 'the figure sees, unseen' (position of social advantage – the man, the author, the spectator), but that 'the figure is looked at, unrecognised' (position of social death). This nonrecognition is the reason that, though appearing to observe the figure in his distress, the other drivers and passengers make no effort to help him. On the contrary, there seems a vague link between the fixity of their stares and the threat of his annihilation. If these others, by virtue of their immobile faces, look like the living dead, ur-Guido figures the undead: an outcast vampire whom the social mirror can't or won't reflect.

Stalled like his car between these two intolerable fates – the social fixity of character and the social marginality of figure – ur-Guido suddenly transcends the dilemma by metamorphosing into a third sort of being: a god who, having escaped his car, ascends into the sky. In this tableau of vehicular gridlock, he has become the only true automobile. We see him rise up from the underpass, above the cars and electric wires; we see him float among sun and clouds;

finally, we simply see the sun and clouds, as though he had turned
into this classic imagery of the divine. Charles Affron sees the cloud
shot as GA's point of view; more faithful to the logic of divine
ascension, I take the shot to register the *disappearance of point of
view* into the objectivity of things as they are. How like a god indeed!
In 1963 GA's ascension would naturally recall the famous opening

images of Fellini's previous film, *La dolce vita* (1959), in which a statue of Christ is being helicoptered across Rome.[5] While Christ, in the frozen form of stone, had to depend on modern technology for his mobility, ur-Guido rises under his own steam; and while that Christ might only look down on immodest bathing beauties or up at cynical pretty boys flirting with them, ur-Guido reaches a state where the toxic vapours he confronted below take the purified form of clouds. The inhumanity of a figure who is visually and socially peripheral has been replaced by the superior inhumanity of a god who is visible only as his creation.

But the body that had been light enough to soar and disappear into the clouds now rematerialises, a rope around its ankle. Like a kite, it may be brought to earth; and when that happens, it all at once acquires the gravity of a lead weight: 'Down, down for good,' says an earthling on the beach who is pulling in the rope; or to translate the Italian literally: 'Down, down *definitively*'. His head no longer in the clouds, ur-Guido falls into what would seem to be definition and death at the same time.

MAN IN THE MIRROR. The tension between character and figure, between the socially abased person and the socially isolated *missing* person, does not disappear when GA wakes up. Waking life carries over the nightmare's dispersion of identity. True, GA wakes up into a world where human kites are impossible; he is only at a spa, about to take the cure. But though being examined by the spa doctor, he remains crucially disembodied, still in shadows or shrouded, his body fragmented into an arm, a leg, the scapula. And even when, in pyjamas, he toddles into a bathroom and looks at himself in the mirror, he remains the facially indistinct figure of

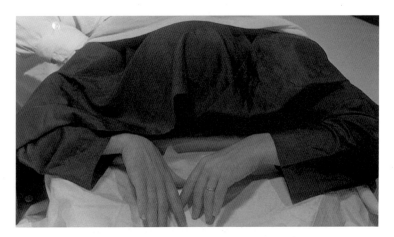

his dream. It is not until he switches on the light above the mirror that he gives us – and himself – a sudden vision of his face. Only now does he seem fully incarnate, the authorial word made characterological flesh.

It used to be common in film to make us wait like this for the face of the star, even a male star, and to hail his eventual appearance with an extreme close-up and something very grand on the soundtrack. Before Montgomery Clift first turns to the camera in *A Place in the Sun* (1951), we have looked at his back throughout the entire opening credits. But when we do finally see him, it is well worth the wait: a full ten seconds of Clift in increasingly tight close-up, while the strings in Franz Waxman's orchestra all rise in salute. But here, on his spectacular emergence from a cocoon of shadows, Marcello Mastroianni seems more a shrunken head than a

countenance in glory. The protocols of fanfare remain – for the first time in the film, we hear music, music no less high-flying than Wagner's 'Ride of the Valkyries' – but they hardly hail a worthy object. Albeit in his prime, Mastroianni disappoints. Scarcely more than a year before, in *Divorce Italian Style* (1961), he had looked at himself in the mirror with a complacency fully justified by the moustached good looks of the man we saw there too. Now, he looks old and tired; his hair is badly greying, and his eyes sag with the sandbags sewn under them. The light is so sudden and intense that it gives him the creepiness of a hospital radiograph. His once classically handsome face has not just aged; it has somehow become damaged, as if its owner had suffered a car accident in fact, or had contracted Fellini-face from the people in his dream. He may not be dead, but he has decidedly come down.

More cruel than the light, moreover, is the sheer brevity of the image. GA quickly turns away, depriving us of any time to reconcile ourselves with his image, to find comforting traces of the old Marcello – that is, the young Marcello – still remaining.[6] And finally, Mastroianni's unfamiliar appearance startles us into realising that, subliminally, we were not expecting him at all; we were expecting *someone else*, someone for whom he is being given us as a substitute. 'What are you cooking up for us,' the doctor had just asked GA, 'another film without hope?' Having been thus primed to expect a celebrated auteur, we are disconcerted to find a well-known actor in his place.

'Would you have been happier with 8½ if Fellini had played it himself?' Peter Bogdanovich once asked Orson Welles, adding: 'I somehow couldn't see Mastroianni as a movie director.'[7] A photograph taken on the set by Tazio Secchiaroli shows Bogdanovich's implicit wish

fulfilled: Mastroianni looks into a mirror that reflects an image of … Fellini. Fellini too must have harboured the wish to 'play it himself'. It is not just that he gave Mastroianni his idiosyncrasies of manner and dress, or that (as Secchiaroli's other on-set photos show), he acted out virtually every scene for his star before it was filmed. In a couple of shots, he literally took over the part. Ur-Guido's tethered leg is, in fact, Fellini's own.[8] And, in a less stealthy arrogation, at the press conference, he has angry reporters yell into his camera while his hero is shown fleeing them in the same shot: GA has been supplanted. But these exceptional moments only reinforce our awareness of the film's otherwise sustained device of representing the auteur *by an actor*. 8½'s mirror scene, unlike Secchiaroli's, does not stage the triumph of the

imaginary. Here, having entrusted his embodiment to an actor, the auteur can no longer say of his mirror-image, 'there I am'; he can no longer say 'I' at all. Like the alien name (GA, not FF), the alien face (MM's, not FF's) consigns him to the third person of fiction: the person as 'he' exists for other characters.[9]

GA too seems to have been expecting to see someone else. If his countenance does not reflect the comfortable self-recognition that a mirror normally affords, neither does it express the horrified aversion that is sometimes the mirror's other face. Instead, it conveys bafflement and disorientation, as though GA had just stepped awkwardly down onto an unfamiliar, differently dimensioned terrain, or even as though he were being subjected for the first time to having dimensions himself. Small wonder that he abruptly turns away: he no longer knows which way to turn, but only knows – this is what it means to be determined as a character – that he can't now turn just anywhere; he is, as we say, in a tight spot. A telephone buzzes in the corner like an emergency alarm, and the harsh light of exposure is suddenly all over the place as an arc light floods the room. If GA is being called to the set, he's also apparently already on it, being filmed. In time to the buzzing, and in reaction to what now seems a permanent state of visibility, he slumps lower and lower, almost down into the indignity of a squat. His declension into the third person has triggered a somatic as well as psychic depression.

Thus does 8½ understand the auteur's cinematic coming out; 'character' is not simply what GA always had or was; it is the new sociobiological condition into which, suddenly and against his will, his godlike being has been shoehorned. His predicament is made the more acute by the fact that, though a neophyte, a recent convert to character, he already bears the body – and all the other baggage – of a forty-three-year-old man. Hence, in protest, the auteur-as-character becomes almost as recessive as the auteur-as-god used to be: unwilling to answer questions, volunteer information, open himself to others. He affects dark glasses to conceal his crow's feet and a black Stetson to hide his more-salt-than-pepper hair. In contrast to the often waxwork poise of other characters, he fidgets, paces, glances away; repeatedly, he walks out of the frame, forcing everyone, including 'his' cameraman, to track him. It is as though, in all this incessant motion, he wanted to leave his new, improperly born body behind for the vagueness of a ghost. 'He's seated himself by the exit,' one character observes of him at a showing of screen tests, 'ready to run off, as usual.'

And his readiness, in this sense, is perfectly matched to his reticence, his fear of definite statement. To all the people who address him (doctors, journalists, his actors and production team), his characteristic response is silence, noncommittal assent or flight across the table, the room, the lobby, the grounds, to another interlocutor doomed to the same frustration. Woody Allen's auteur-surrogate, Sandy Bates, will chatter nonstop throughout *Stardust*

Memories (1980), and not the least obscene adventure in *Super 8½* (1993), Bruce La Bruce's art-porn *hommage* to Fellini, will be La Bruce's uncensored love affair with the languorous sound of his own voice. But GA, the model for these author-heroes, holds his tongue to the point of mutism. His original resistance to being a character in the nightmare persists in character traits of diffidence, indecision, irritability and mendacity, traits by which he continues to deny his fall into the realm of physical restrictions and social determinations.

All this gets continually reinforced by Mastroianni's particular qualities as an actor. Fellini justly praised Mastroianni for his extraordinary *disponibilità* – his uninhibited openness to the maestro's instructions and cues. Elsewhere, this suggestibility allowed him to be that rare thing in a star, a character actor; in the course of his long career, he could play a taxi driver (in *Too Bad She's Bad* [1954]) or a petty crook (in *Big Deal on Madonna Street* [1958]), an alienated intellectual (in *La notte* [1961]) or a shy homosexual (in *A Special Day* [1977]), with equal conviction. But, as Fellini well understood, Mastroianni's sheer versatility implies something provisional, revocable, about his commitment to a role; the experimental ease with which he tries on moods and attitudes also involves a readiness to abandon them for others when the wind shifts. What makes his performance in *8½* the most definitive of his talent is that here *he plays his own latency*; rather than impersonate somebody in particular, he conveys an embryonic condition from which any number of individuals might issue forth. But not one ever does: with his self-abstracted face and carriage, he has held character development in perpetual abeyance. We can never be sure whether his GA is brooding or benumbed, whether he hides secret depths or the secret shallowness of such depths. In this indeterminacy, Mastroianni remains the very opposite of a character: an actor, a vessel.

THESIS. In a word, if Fellini's famous self-incarnation sins against good authorship, it fails to sin boldly; it happens but half-heartedly, only more or less. What mars it is less self-indulgence than a failure of nerve, an exhibitionism that somehow (for reasons we will see) lacks the courage of its conviction. And the fictive auteur's uncomfortable relation to embodiment doubles the real auteur's skittish relation to his film's own conceit. FF can never decide whether to 'be' GA or to 'see' GA, whether to make him an 'I' who is identified with the camera's own act of seeing or a 'he' who has been placed instead under its critical surveillance. When god becomes man in 8½, he doesn't become man enough; and having once engaged the process of placing – and hence limiting – his perspective in a character, he no longer quite remains a god. What has been widely denounced as GA/FF's self-indulgence is just this disappointing (even infuriating) double humility.

2 From Auteur to Person

ON THE BEACH WITH BEN-HUR. Postponements, casting problems, overrun budgets – but GA is not filming *Cleopatra*, which, like *8½*, was being made in Rome in 1962. What *is* this blockbuster on which he finds himself blocked? Here is his producer, Pace (Guido Albertini), describing its 'most important scene' to visitors on a tour of the set:

The sequence begins with a view of planet Earth completely destroyed by a thermonuclear war. There appears a true Noah's ark ... the spaceship that tries to escape the atomic plague. What remains of humanity looks for a safe haven on another planet. More than 10,000 extras ... maybe 15,000! You understand ... a tragic crowd that abandons forever ...

The grandiosity of this summary, already impressive, is amplified by the evidence before our eyes. The set on which Pace holds forth is a skyscraper of scaffolding whose erection has cost 80 million lire and required 400 tons of reinforced concrete. When special effects superimpose a model over it, it will be the spaceship's launching pad. At the base, we see this model displayed – looking, Hiroshima

notwithstanding, like vintage *Flash Gordon* – along with a
composite photograph, printed on a large cloth screen, suggesting
that the 'tragic crowd' will be led to the spaceship by the Pope
himself, complete with throne, baldochin, Egyptian fans, Swiss
Guards and Risorgimento carabinieri.

Like its set, GA's bizarre science fiction is torn between the
monumental and the minimal. Is it whoring after the megalithic
materiality of the Hollywood-on-the-Tiber spectacular? Or aspiring
to take its place amid the gaunt after-the-bomb allegories favoured by
Bergman, Kurosawa and other 'serious' film-makers? In the battle for
its soul, William Wyler's *Ben-Hur* (1959) seems to be warring with
Stanley Kramer's *On the Beach* (1959). Yet bewildered though the
project may be, its gigantism ensures one certitude: a total eclipse of
the individual. If anyone manages not to get lost amid the cast of
thousands thronging the supersized set, he will surely disappear in the
spaced-out abstractions of a 'humanity' that inhabits 'planet Earth'

and whose spirituality takes the equally universal form – in Italy at any rate – of a Catholic Church. Indeed, whether in the crowd or in the stars, why speak of getting lost at all, when GA's film has dispensed with the very notion of a protagonist? There is only one means by which an individual could attract serious notice in this project, and this is the ridicule that so much kitsch must visit upon its originator.

The ridicule begins, lightly enough, as soon as Rossella (Rossella Falk), the spiritualist friend of GA's wife, Luisa (Anouk Aimée), has overheard Pace's summary. 'Are you really putting all that in your film?' she asks GA. 'Mamma mia! The prophet is speaking at full volume.' GA offers an irked defence – 'Do you like stories where nothing happens? In my film, everything happens!' – but finally concedes that all his generalities cover a total blank: 'I have really nothing to say ... but I want to say it anyway.' Though he declaims this *cri de coeur* in a self-mocking singsong, it is, I think, the most important statement made in 8½; the entire film may be understood as a gradual unpacking of the ambiguities and paradoxes condensed in it. Even from the start, however, we grasp the implicit scandal of GA's words; uttered by a Hollywood hack, they would pass for the cynical perception of business as usual; but spoken by an auteur, who, in contradistinction to the hack, is supposed to have 'something to say', they have the potential to shock and outrage the whole organised cultural field.

THE PRESS CONFERENCE. At the press conference called to launch the film (where else but at the launching pad), this potential is realised to the point of mass hysteria. The sequence begins with precisely inverted reminders of the anxiety-dream that opened the film. There the cars were stalled; here the motorcade taking GA to the set proceeds apace. Then the others were unresponsive to GA; now they concentrate on him alone, guarding, greeting, grilling him. And whereas the traffic jam was only orchestrated by the muffled drum of GA's heartbeat, the press conference unfolds to the quickest, most piercing music in Nino Rota's score, his version of the 'Sabre Dance'. These contrasts, we're to understand, simply highlight GA's tongue-tied paralysis in both sequences. For the press conference obeys the logic of a nightmare, too: the kind in which you find yourself having to make an important speech that you've somehow neglected to write. No sooner has GA realised that 'there isn't even a film' than he is forcibly enlisted – press-ganged, we might say – into promoting and defending it.

'Are you for or against eroticism?' 'Are you afraid of the atomic bomb?' 'Do you, or don't you, believe in God?' 'Are you for or against divorce?' 'Do you think that pornography is an art form?' 'Why don't you make a film about love?' As GA makes no answer to the myriad questions thrown at him by the press, 'I have nothing to say' becomes his literal truth. His silence only provokes the journalists; to break it – or, failing that, to break him – they become strident, manic, vicious. Led on by its most rabid members (mainly women: the Furies), the entire press corps eventually storms the dais. 'He's lost,' shrills a Fury for all to hear, baring her teeth the better to castrate with, 'he has *nothing* to say!' Though she echoes GA's own words to Rossella, these no longer bespeak an alterable subjective state; they certify a decisive objective fact: the scandal of the 'nothing to say' has become public. Pointedly, the Fury speaks these words in English, a language that GA understands but cannot speak: a finishing touch to the unbearable mortification of his life in the third person.

In the shooting script for 8½, the collective violence went as far as an actual lynching. In the finished film, it merely drives GA under the table to shoot himself. What does GA in is not just the Furies or even the press, but the united pressure of the cultural field at large. On behalf of the field's material wing, Pace couldn't be more direct: 'Speak or I'll ruin you.' And it is Daumier (Jean Rougeul), the high intellectual brought in to be GA's collaborator and critic, who incites his mass-media confrères to their first show of aggression. A quick close-up has shown him craning in the direction of the journalists, with a glance that seems to be a signal. In apparent response, the

suddenly restive journalists start to wave angry pencils at GA, as if preparing to accompany their pointed questions with literal darts. Then a second quick shot shows Daumier turning back, his ascetic countenance lit up with secret gratification that his scorn for GA has become communal property. Even after the press conference – for GA hasn't died; he has merely woken up to a world in which there is no longer a film to make – Daumier continues pontificating against a project that has lacked intellectual rationale: 'There are already too many superfluous things in the world. It's not a good idea to add more disorder to disorder. ... It's better to destroy than to create when you're not creating those few things that are truly necessary.'

It is understandable why the journalists, other-directed hacks, should be infuriated by GA's mutism; unless this self-directed artist provides them with something to say, they are in the professionally catastrophic position of having nothing to say themselves. It is equally obvious why Daumier, the Antonioniesque intellectual, should seek to bring on a debacle that confirms his austere doctrine of justification.[10] But it is puzzling why GA stays silent. After all, no matter how cruel or intractable, the demand to 'say something' is also quite easily satisfied. In the world of cultural journalism, what one 'has to say' doesn't have to be particularly smart or original; indeed, given that it must be culled from a dictionary of received ideas, it can *never* be these things. As Conocchia (Mario Conocchia) whispers to GA on the dais, 'Say something – anything at all! Say anything at all!' That is in essence what, less kindly, the journalists have been telling him all along. 'Are you for or against X? Do you believe in Y? Are you, or aren't you, Z?' Despite superficial variety, their questions repeat the same request: that GA position himself in current cultural opinion – that he be, in this sense, *sociable*. Let him say he is a Marxist, a Catholic, an existentialist, some hybrid of these eminently circulable identities; let him say he believes in God, divorce, eroticism, nuclear disarmament, commissioned works of art, or that he *doesn't* believe in these things. He need only take a position – any of the ones currently certified to count will do – and he will be socially saved; his work will matter, and he will matter along with it.

Yet GA does not comply. Throughout this phony war of ideas, he perseveres in a kind of conscientious objection, and with the second half of his statement to Rossella, his resistance loses even the veneer of passivity: 'But I want to say it anyway.' Having abdicated his regal duty as *regista*, he dares retain the throne, his wilfulness in direct proportion to its lack of raison d'être. But supposing his profession of incompetence were a disguised form of that duty? One journalist, cleverer than the rest, broaches the possibility that there is a message in GA's mutism: 'Is that your basic problem,' he asks, 'that you cannot communicate – or is that just a pretext?' Perhaps, with his stammering and his silence, GA is not embracing a fate, so much as pursuing a tactic. But to what strategy would the tactic belong? If 'I have nothing to say' is counter-factual, how may we understand its irony? Here are some first answers; others will be forthcoming.

THREE RHETORICS OF NOTHING. Even if, quite simply, we take 'nothing' to mean *nothing* – the zero-degree of artistic statement – it has to mean more than that: 'I want to say it anyway.' So aggressively does GA embrace his discursive vacuity that it amounts to an actual purpose: to blight the culture machine with crazy-making sterility. In this sense, GA is less in crisis than *on strike*, and his silence not only withdraws him from the stupid but insistent game of ideological position-taking that is all the press conference knows of artistic creation; it also rather slyly exposes the game as such. Without his belief or participation, it seems *only* a game: factitious, superficial, having no more important intellectual aim than to keep itself going. 'I have nothing to say' would be the watchword of his protest against mass culture, the media and the whole ideological polarisation of postwar Italy, with its stultifying culture wars between the Communist Party and the Church. What makes this resistance particularly heroic is the dismal prospect that, between the force of ideologisation (politics) and the technology of garrulity (the media), having nothing to say *may no longer be possible*; and even if it were, little time would be lost – consider the promptness of the clever journalist's question – before the refusal of ideology became the sign of itself, an ideology of refusal. So as not to solidify into 'something', into another *idée reçue*, GA's 'nothing' can only endure by vanishing into utter nonentity; ironically, the success of intellectual resistance requires the failure of artistic realisation. This is, of course, just what happens after the catastrophe of the press conference: production is called off. While the set is being dismantled, Daumier commends GA for the admirable high-modernist logic of his position:

Today is a good day for you. ... I congratulate you! ... It's better to knock it all down and strew the ground with salt, as the ancients did, to purify their battlefields. ... What we really need is some hygiene, some cleanliness, some disinfection. ... Anyone who deserves to be called an artist should be asked to make this single act of faith: to educate oneself to silence. Do you remember Mallarmé's praise of the blank page? And Rimbaud ... do you know what his finest poetry was? His refusal to continue writing and his departure for Africa. ... Nothingness is the real perfection.

By his artistic martyrdom, GA would finally be exemplifying true intellectual austerity.

But 8½ does not end with this act of *démontage*, nor do we expect it to. We've seen too many Hollywood stories of the artist genius not to know that, though his story makes a requisite stop in Gethsemane, where inspiration forsakes him, it doesn't remain there for good. After all, GA has acquired international renown precisely by virtue of making films that had a lot to say for themselves or (what in ideologised culture comes to the same thing) had a lot said about them. 'What are you cooking up for us – another film without hope?' Thus the spa doctor seemed to allude to *La dolce vita*, a film with something to say if ever there were; bearing on celebrity culture and the emerging mass media, on the economic miracle and sexual modernism, on all these things vis-à-vis the Church, its message threw an entire nation into debate. After such success, in any case, GA is not looking to continue his career, but to crown it, and the laurels will not be owing to another work with something to say, but to a summa that says it all. If it is highly improbable that the 'nothing' of this artist genius could ever mean literally *nothing*, it is equally unlikely that his 'nothing' could mean *something*, in the sense of Conocchia's 'anything'. What GA pretends is a total blank is, in fact, the blank he is reserving for totality; 'nothing' is his interim place-holder for *everything*. 'I'm putting everything in,' he has told Rossella, 'even the sailor doing the tap dance'; the pathetic-seeming embrace of miscellany already adumbrates the higher ambition to all-inclusiveness. 'If you can't have everything,' Daumier will later declare, 'then nothing is the real perfection'; but if, like GA, you won't have 'nothing', then 'everything' is the best alternative. 'But I want to say it anyway': so GA declares his determination to persevere in biding his time until such comprehensive illumination of life and art be granted him. It is this saving grace that seems to descend on him at the end; and when at last he resumes his megaphone, we understand (whatever we think of *8½*: the understanding is structural, not evaluative) that he is not simply shooting a film, he is making a masterpiece.

Finally, besides the rhetoric of refusal and the rhetoric of genius, there is a third, far more mundane rhetoric that speaks through GA's words: that of coquetry. In this rhetoric, 'I have nothing to say' is a shy formula for soliciting the quasi-maternal assurance: 'But of course you do.' More: the formula designates not just content 'after all', but a new, original content, a content outside the customary range of things that cultural producers are supposed to have-to-say; neither nothing nor everything, it is, simply, *something else*. In this sense, GA is neither the noncompliant intellectual ('I will not speak') nor the struggling genius ('I am waiting to speak'), but a practising auteur: 'I am already speaking, but I am saying something different; will it be heard?'[11] What is this something else, this difference, that GA, the better to get it a hearing, modestly calls 'nothing'?

I, GUIDO. Most viewers of *8½* do not have so defined an impression of GA's sci-fi film as the one I've given; that is because all our information about this film comes to us while our attention is being claimed by just this something else. Pace's plot summary, for instance, is merely overheard by Rossella as she is talking to GA about Luisa's unhappiness. Likewise, as we see the photograph of the Pope leading

the people into the spaceship, we also see – larger, starker, considerably more cinematic – the shadow of Luisa crossing behind the canvas screen on which it's been printed. The image graphically reminds us that behind the film GA is making stands another film, a shadow film *that he is also making*. If the authorised film deserves to be called 'On the Beach with Ben-Hur', this shadow film might be entitled 'I, Guido', for it centres exclusively on GA the person. In contrast to 'On the Beach with Ben-Hur', which is nothing but generality, 'I, Guido' is all particularity. It examines everything about GA, from his body's petty disorder ('the liver') to his soul's grand confusion (the Church). It treats his women problems – with Luisa, with his mistress, Carla (Sandra Milo), with a host of other 'other women' – as well as his guarded, testy relations with men friends and collaborators. It follows his memory into the past, back to childhood baths, Catholic school and Saraghina (Edra Gale), the *mamma puttana* who initiated him sexually. It tracks his dreams – ascending above a traffic jam, meeting his dead father – and even his daydreams as they weave fantasy solutions to his waking predicaments: a woman in white who would bring purity and harmony in her train; a harem where all his women would live in peace; a summary execution that would prevent Daumier from making further criticisms; and a suicide that would get him out of everything.

'On the Beach with Ben-Hur' never gets beyond a set and a summary. By contrast, the director of 'I, Guido' has already written a detailed treatment, which is being vetted by Daumier and even a representative of the Church; screen tests have been done for some roles, and the casting of others is visibly in process. In this film, the answer to the riddle of GA's 'nothing to say' is himself, and his project, far from being a blank, is no more arcane than autobiography. 'All this confusion is me, myself'; this is the ungeneric subject that must and will be filmed. To the extent that 8½ has a plot, it is usually thought to consist in GA's final shift from the manifest sci-fi film, which ends in catastrophe at the press conference, to the latent autobiographical film, which has been engaging his deeper energies for work all along. We seem to move from a negative confusion to a positive one, from intellectual vacuity to an inexhaustible personal totality: '*All* this confusion is me.' On the basis of this understanding, 8½ has inspired several generations of personal film-makers.

TROUBLE WITH SELF-INDULGENCE. In the sharp eyes of Daumier, however, autobiography and 'nothing to say' amount to the same thing. As he remarks to GA apropos of the Saraghina episode: 'What does it mean? It's a character from your childhood. It has nothing to do with a true critical consciousness.' And more generally: 'What a monstrous presumption to think that others might enjoy the squalid catalogue of your mistakes!' The personal means nothing if it doesn't acquire critical consciousness and thereby rise to social representativeness. Following the cue of their high priest in this too, the journalists cast his point into their more vulgarly moralistic idiom: 'Aren't you taking yourself a bit too seriously?' one Fury asks (in English here too), while another demands: 'Do you really think that your life can be of interest to others?' Already, the charge of self-indulgence that Fellini's critics would level against 8½ is being prophesied in the accusations made against GA.[12]

The charge, then, seems somewhat gratuitous. One of the main meanings of *confusione* in Italian is embarrassment or shame, and GA is already abundantly 'confused' in this sense as well. From the start, as we've seen, the auteur has undertaken his self-representation with reluctance, and this reluctance presupposes a certain humiliation attendant on personal incarnation. In the broad sense given in the opening nightmare, humiliation is part of our general fate as social beings; despite ourselves, a social text (of names, attributes, valuations) gets written on our face as soon as we enter the third person. But now, as the nightmare yields to the waking world where GA is a forty-three-year-old man with a wife, a mistress, a liver problem and a film to make, generic humiliation gets itemised in some highly particular ignominies. 'The world is "insulting",' says Didier Eribon, 'because it is structured according to hierarchies, which carry with them the possibility of insult.'[13] From what positions does GA – who is, after all, a famous high-cultural producer – anticipate such possibility? What species of damage are his?

A COMIC FILM. For one thing, though GA has become a character, he's not in much of a plot. That is the nature of midlife crisis: the great adventures of social life (love, ambition) are over, and their main outcomes (marriage, profession) have taken place. Even in the biological sense, the life-story has come to a tedious passage. Fellini insisted at the start that it be 'a not so serious illness' that brings GA to the spa – not a death sentence, but a minor ailment announcing a mortality still far off. Its message is more spiteful than fatal: *just you wait*. Midlife 'crisis'? If only (we imagine GA sighing) his state *were* a crisis – a narrative peak, a recognition, a reversal, a knot that would require denouement; if only, on the contrary, it didn't seem to name a shift from the very realm of plot to an unvaliant new world of mere incident. Once begun, the so-called crisis seems endless; like the ailment that brings it about, it promises a chronic condition that must be 'managed' with makeshifts and compromises until the end of his days.

The pitiful (less pathetic than paltry) story of male midlife is hardly one that our culture welcomes. It is deficient in the traditional exploits by which we measure a man or build a civilisation with him. Unconcerned with the couple of reproduction, it is unnecessary for our survival; and indifferent to the child of the future, it is bad for our morale. The Fury is exactly right: *it has nothing to teach us.* Since 8½, we no longer altogether censor this story – which now ekes out a demeaning existence as a minor Hollywood genre – but we obviously still meet it with censure, snorting outright at the 'sentimentality' to which, apparently, only more favoured tales of love or coming-of-age are entitled. As the Furies' prominence here suggests, this condemnation is most persuasive coming from a

woman, who inevitably inflects it with sexual contempt. But middle-aged men, too, have little respect for their climacteric: Pace, Daumier and Mezzabotta (Mario Pisu) are each too busy making a separate peace with his condition to have any fellow-feeling for GA's. The only acceptable means of treating so ridiculous a story is comedy, comedy broad enough to legitimise ridicule as our genre-given right. Fellini fully understood this, his treatment drawing copiously on French farce, Italian music hall and Mack Sennett, to assure the cultural welcome of his hero's funny-very-funny story. On his camera, he even attached a note to himself saying, 'Remember, this is a comic film.' The reminder was, as we say, painfully necessary.

THE UNGENITOR. If GA had fallen to his death in the opening sequence, his gold wedding band would probably be the only thing that would allow forensic medicine to identify him. This ring, already visible in his nightmare, becomes so conspicuous in the medical examination (though we still haven't seen GA's face) that it provides, with his gender, the first index of his social identity. The ring never leaves his finger (a detail made pertinent by the fact that Carla is often misplacing hers). Yet this insistent badge of GA's fundamental social integration is also always the brand of a certain social failure – of a deep, deeply denied shame.

Something about this marriage hasn't taken. 'You two have been the joy of my life,' GA's father (Annibale Ninchi) tells him from beyond the grave; but a guilt-trip lies behind the fulsome paternal approval, for Papa suspects a different truth: 'And with your wife … is everything all right?' It isn't just that GA's marriage, now twenty years old, has achieved its pluperfect form in adultery, or that his established mistress has become as nagging as the wife from whom she thus prevents him from imagining the point of a separation. GA's sexual preferences have never been socially acceptable: the chthonic Saraghina has been succeeded by the merely vulgar Carla, whom, even as Saraghina Lite, he is ashamed to admit into his circle. Conversely, his marital choice – the elegant, class-appropriate Luisa –

inspires him neither sexually nor professionally.[14] Just before his 'suicide' at the press conference, GA imagines her reproaching him, still in her bridal gown: 'When will you truly marry me?' It is as though the marriage hadn't yet been consummated.

In the deepest social-symbolic sense, this is exactly the case. Hear GA in conversation with the Church Cardinal (Tito Masini) whom he has arranged to meet at the spa:

CARDINAL   Are you married?

GA   Yes.

CARDINAL   Do you have children?

GA   Yes ... I mean, no.

CARDINAL   How old are you?

GA   Forty-three.

The conversation ends here; the Cardinal has made his point: married, GA does not have children – a fact that his age, or perhaps what it suggests about Luisa's, seems to render an inalterable fate. For a moment, under pressure of inquisition, GA can't quite admit this; like a closeted homosexual who makes up a long-distance girlfriend, he finds himself inventing an imaginary child.[15] His slip – 'Yes ... I mean, no' – only underscores the stress of stigma from which he suffers as a confirmed ungenitor.[16] In 1963 Italy, without divorce or abortion, the Cardinal can hardly be speaking simply for the Church, whose doctrines on marriage and sexuality informed state law as well as social norm. Even now, in Italy or anywhere else, the Cardinal's first two questions – Are you married? Do you have children? – touch so basically on social existence that they are equally at home on a dental insurance form as in the mouth of a prince of the Church. They amount to a public test – it is still *the* test – of a person's mature socialisation. Albeit famous for womanising, GA has failed at heterosexuality's social vocation: to turn copulation into a couple and this couple into parents of a child.

MARIO MEZZABOTTA, 96 KILOGRAMS. For the same reasons that
GA is uneasy in his skin, Mario Mezzabotta, the old friend whom
he runs into at the spa, is healthy, cheerful and abundantly self-
satisfied. At first, GA takes his young female companion for his
daughter ('My, how she has grown!'); in fact, she used to be his
daughter's schoolmate. But Gloria (Barbara Steele), though she
bears the same name as the society whore in Antonioni's
L'avventura (1960), is no bimbo-in-waiting; Mezzabotta intends to
make her his lawful wife as soon as the Church annuls his marriage.
What she offers him, dearer than sex (if obviously including it), is
the opportunity to reenact the plot of youth – couple and family
formation – and reacquire the social currency enjoyed by its
protagonists. He's not so much in his second childhood as in his
second parenthood – Gloria being thirty years his junior and prone
to tantrums – and it is likely that he will enter a third once her
biological clock rings the alarm. Gloria is the 'child' who has
reached child-bearing age; in proximity to this double figure of 'new
generation', Mezzabotta expects to revitalise his middle years.

His is the classic resolution to male midlife crisis. Everything
about this outcome is a cliché, from its overstated symbolism (see
Gloria, like a young woman in late Ibsen, pop a spring cherry into
Mezzabotta's mouth) to its disingenuous rationalisation ('Ah, my wife
took it badly; Gloria, poor thing, is actually quite fond of her'). But
Mezzabotta is not one whom the obvious much embarrasses; if subtlety
and good faith are the eggs he has had to break for his omelette, the
benefits of the dish are incontestable. He is all over Gloria with public
kisses and embraces, and he gamely, if awkwardly, joins her in the latest
dance craze (minor, but sublime pleasure of 8½: Barbara Steele doing
the twist). His extended youth is not without qualification: his efforts
on the dance floor throw him into a visible sweat; and, at the mud
baths, the labour of sheer breathing keeps him from answering GA's
greeting, or even recognising him, as though he were on the verge of a
stroke. But such ironies belong to the physical realm; socially speaking,
Mezzabotta exudes the confidence of someone with the right relation to

the married-with-children requirement of socialisation. Long ago able
to answer the Cardinal's questions without confusion, he wants nothing
better than to be his compliant catechumen once more. In return, the
Church will grant him an annulment as surely as it did to Carlo Ponti,
whose liaison with Sophia Loren is Fellini's model here. 'Mario
Mezzabotta,' he introduces himself, '96 kilograms' (212 pounds); like
many such men, he's secretly proud of being fat; it speaks to his solidity.

THE HAREM. By contrast, no pervert could feel guiltier than GA
does about his correctly oriented, but unacceptably futile sexuality.
This is why even GA's harem fantasy ends up being so melancholy.
It doesn't, of course, begin that way. Having braved the blizzard
raging outdoors, GA enters the seraglio laden with presents – an
alpha male who can and does deliver the goods. Collected inside is
almost every female of his personal, professional and even passing

acquaintance; each receives her present with delighted appreciation, and all are eager to serve and obey. The only cloud on their horizon is the prospect of being sent 'upstairs' after a certain age, where they will live outside the radar of GA's sexual interest. Otherwise, Luisa, Carla, Gloria, Rossella, the uncast French actress (Madeleine LeBeau), the seamstress from his production office (Grazia Frasnelli), the older beauty spotted at the hotel (Caterina Boratto), the aging showgirl (Yvonne Casadei), the Scandinavian stewardess (Nadine Sanders), the black dancer (Hazel Rogers), even his snide sister-in-law (Elisabetta Catalano) – all dwell in a harmony secured by their common interest in looking after their man-master, perfectly accepting that (as Luisa puts it) 'things have to be like this.'

GA's oriental despotism is quartered in a farmhouse that is as far away from the world as a Sadean chateau or an early bordello (from French *borde*, small farm). However, it also happens to be the farmhouse of his childhood memories, and among the concubines, a couple of Boy Guido's former nannies have remained on the premises. The association suggests that what goes on in the harem isn't all that 'adult'. GA has had sex with some of these women in the past, and he might have sex with others in the future; but at present – during the time of the fantasy's actual unfolding – his concubines' principal task, supervised by the nannies whom we've seen at this work before, is to give him a bath. They regard his nakedness serenely, Saraghina remarking that his legs haven't changed since he was a boy. Our hero even lacks body hair; Fellini had Mastroianni shave his chest, so as to suggest the glabrous immaturity of 'a big baby with diaper rash'.[17]

'Tell me, Guido,' asks Rossella, voicing the anxiety he ought to be feeling, 'Aren't you a bit afraid?' 'Afraid of what?' he retorts blankly, still unaware that the double valence of his harem/nursery implies, beneath the surface male domination, a perhaps more fundamental matriarchy. He loses his naiveté when the overage showgirl refuses to be sent upstairs; the same women who a moment before had been giving him adoring looks now rise up in mutinous solidarity. They justify their revolt not just on feminist grounds of unfairness – though Saraghina bellows the obvious point: '*Non è giusto!*' – but also from the more traditional, but infinitely more cruel, female perspective of sheer disappointment. 'Let's say it once and for all,' says the showgirl, 'he doesn't know how to make love. Caresses and talk – that's all.' The French actress seconds her: 'He falls asleep right afterward.' It is hard being a good patriarch – God knows – but GA blows even the fun part. All his presents haven't been enough to buy off the transference of the women's humiliation onto him, as the personification of fiasco. In France, the actress tells him, he would be 'the disgrace of the nation'; even in his fantasy life, GA must experience his Don Juanism as a social pathology, complete with the impotence that is widely considered its just deserts. He comes to resemble not a sultan, but the other man whom custom lets enter the seraglio: the eunuch.

At this juncture, GA reaches for a whip and, amid shrieks and flying feathers, eventually subdues his rioting womankind. But the harem's ambiguity undercuts even this brutal display. Is it a triumph? And if so, whose? Saraghina squares off as if welcoming the challenge, Gloria positively thrills to the lash ('delicious!'), and Carla is laughing even as she flees its application. At the end of his labours, the women applaud as though this were another of GA's 'performances'; granted, it is more satisfying than the ones they've been complaining about – he's mighty cute when he's angry – but it is to be taken no more seriously. That is why Luisa has felt free to interrupt it with a mundane reminder that the soup is getting cold; and why now, at its close, she comments on it with similarly maternal condescension: 'He needs to act like this. He does it every night.' But the nightly outburst, compulsively repeated in place of the no longer practicable sex act, brings no relief, let alone pleasure. Despite the apparent restoration of his kingdom, the sovereign does not return to the sweetness of living before the revolution. 'What's wrong?' he asks himself. 'Why this sadness?'

Why indeed? The scene's last image shows Luisa, alone under a spotlight, scrubbing the floor on hands and knees, while she cheerfully inventories for GA the chores she must complete before she sleeps: the laundry, the dishes, the floors, the mending, the preparations for tomorrow's breakfast. 'You see, Guido, how good I've become. I don't pester you any more. I don't ask you for anything.' But she might as well be weeping with shame and mortification (as she does in the shooting script); GA does not share her contentment, nor does her transformation into a patient, all-accepting mother comfort him. On the contrary, the more Luisa goes on in this vein, the more he feels guilty, to the point where he is shaken out of his daydream altogether. It is as though Luisa as 'mother' were an unbearable reminder that he has usurped the place of the child he ought to have sired. Her sweet-tempered prompt here – 'Do you remember the day we got married?' – anticipates the more open form of reproach at the press conference: 'When will you truly make me your wife?' Acme of wish fulfilment, the harem is sad, the way households without children are said to be.

THESIS. However fertile in fantasies, GA's imagination works at a single task, which is to cover the stigma of his 'bad' social-symbolic relation to the 'woman' and the 'child'. The harem fantasy scorned that stigma for an alternative reality, or tried to, before it collapsed into a scene of abjection so intolerable that GA had to leave the stage to Luisa. On other tracks of his mind, however, he is more directly reparative, busy fantasising that 'good' relation to the 'woman' and the 'child', which would make him feel right about himself.

AQUARIA. At the spa, for instance, his fantasy materialises a beautiful young woman who, clad in the all-white uniform worn by the nurses and attendants, approaches him with a glass of mineral water. It is as if, by some hidden conduit, the healing properties of this Happy Water (as we are told the ancient Romans called this spring) had been transferred to her smiling face and just-ripened body, where they no longer admitted misgivings! This well-aspected maiden of the spring

has no name, but as she bears a water glass – thus allegorising the birth-sign of the superstitious Fellini (born 20 January) as well as the then-dawning astrological age of spiritual renewal – let us call her Aquaria. Along with the limpid waters, Aquaria offers the transparency of her own symbolism. She would clearly be a sort of glorified Gloria, reviving GA in ways better suited to his more distinguished standing. (Gloria is merely getting her degree in philosophy; Aquaria is in training to be a muse.) If we have failed to grasp this symbolism on its first apparition, GA obligingly glosses it later as 'purity' and 'innocence'; and should we have missed even this explication, which he offers more than once, Aquaria herself is as ready to expound her mission as a broken record: 'I want to bring order, cleansing, order, cleansing.' In the harem scene, unsurprisingly, she is conspicuous by her absence.

For most viewers, this blatancy is a blemish: 'Some muse! She has inspired GA to forget the first rule of the art film!' There, as is well known, the symbol is required to possess a certain density, a kind of obscurity that may not see light of day without strenuous mental midwifery. That the overwrought Aquaria just *isn't working* becomes literal fact when, in a later daydream, she is shown perusing GA's script – as reverentially as she might turn over the pages of an illuminated manuscript – and then breaking out of role into open-mouthed laughter. Even she finds her symbolism ridiculous. 'You're right,' GA glumly concurs. And Daumier had already weighed in: 'Of all the symbols that abound in your story, this is the worst!'

If Aquaria is a bad idea, then it is (like so many other critically identified flaws in 8½) one that the film foregrounds as such, treating it to a whole range of sabotaging ironies. The most basic irony, of course, is that Aquaria is played by an actress, Claudia Cardinale, whose devastatingly sensual beauty is the least likely to escort anyone, Beatrice-like, to the higher signifieds. Granted, la Cardinale's gracefully curved body is too wanting in starch to seem 'built' like that of the period's natural-born sexpots or their siliconed successors today; but it becomes all the more essentially fleshly for not seeming to have a bone in it. Her face, too – soft, round, heavy – lacks that sculptural emphasis that cinema resorts to when it wants to denote a woman of 'character'. Her eyes, dark enough to look black, sparkle with joy, or flash with passion, but never pierce with truth; and her mouth, overwide for classic proportion, smacks largely of appetite. In the very heyday of hairspray, her early-60s coiffure is always a touch dishevelled, as though to mark her resplendent carnality with the sign of someone's inevitable 'knowledge' of it. To complete this overall inappropriateness, Fellini has let her keep her own voice, whose raspy grain, as unsuitable in a conduit as in a woman, had always before been dubbed.

Aquaria-as-Cardinale turns Aquaria-as-Beatrice into a camp as solemn and giggly-making as a Symbolist play.[18] It comes as a relief to see her, after GA has gone on about 'the lure of purity', stripped down to a slip. But the relief too is comic; when her sexuality is finally taken out from under its new-age wraps, this Sacred Prostitute starts resembling a prostitute *tout court*, with a bedroom look straight out of Carla's repertory. Nor are we are done yet: this symbol of purity and innocence keeps on failing, in more and different ways. As 'Claudia', the actress who is supposed to play Aquaria, Cardinale seems even less right for the part, wearing a black outfit with feathers, and accompanied by a look-alike secretary who only speaks English. GA's meeting with Claudia goes badly, each party irritated

by an incompatibility that neither had expected. From him: 'You're a
bit of a bore, like the others'; and from her: 'You look like an old
man' who – she repeats this three times, like a spell – 'doesn't know
how to love.' We are back in the harem. (We are also back,
intertextually, in Mauro Bolognini's *Il bell'Antonio* [1960], where
Mastroianni, the titular Casanova, is unable to make love to
Cardinale, his newly wedded wife.) The Aquarian fantasy of
redemption, like the harem fantasy of defiance, ends up reviving all
the confusion of GA's shame. Here, too, he wants only to disappear,
this time taking the film along with him. 'There's no part in the film.
There's not even a film. There's nothing at all. As far as I'm
concerned, the whole thing can end right here.' And it does; what
follows is the press conference and his suicide.

Yet the suicide, we know, somehow 'un-happens', just as the
film's cancellation is itself rescinded. Aquaria's dismissal may be

likewise revocable. Though she was always an obviously bad idea, GA has taken a long time – almost the length of the film – to reject her; even having done so, will he ever get over her? The doubt is allowable; she is, after all, already a revenant, a belated appearance of the Umbrian Angel who had beckoned the hero at the end of *La dolce vita*. In that film, too, she was ultimately dismissed, but only, apparently, to return in this one, where no amount of irony is able to curtail the repetitive, stupid, boring and pointless ongoingness of GA's weirdly loving relation to her. Behind GA's reluctance to become a character lies the bathetic *persistence* of character in reenacting, again and again, its psychosocial fate; that is what, among other things, the reluctance is a fear of showing. Like the homosexual who keeps forming 'crushes' on women, too blinded by the thrill of normality to see the calamitous or anticlimactic outcome that is part and parcel of his infatuations, so GA broods over Aquaria's symbolic function not to make it clear – he is not addressing himself to fools – but to make it real. And just as those hapless crushes never work out, this ill-starred dream of GA's keeps being revealed as nothing more than his insane desire to realise it, an evergreen dead end.

BOY GUIDO. If GA cannot base a future on a child he doesn't have, he can and does mine his past in search of a wholeness that he hopes to recover through the child he once was. 'Where did I go wrong?' GA wonders; his inner child might prove a useful means of answering this question, of establishing an original simplicity before the straight way was lost in the midlife wilderness. Being simple, after all, is supposed to be the child's great privilege. And that simplicity, regained, might ground a self-acceptance that would let him look at the others, as he says to Luisa, 'without shame'.

Yet even in the first childhood episode – Boy Guido (Riccardo Guglielmi) is given a wine bath and afterwards put to bed – the emphasis is placed on an all-entwining sensuousness that already promises plenty of complications. The luminous vision of childhood has perhaps never found a better cinematic exemplar. Whether hopping in the tub or slithering along the floor, with quivering shoulders or wriggling limbs, this boy is quite literally vibrant with his impressions of the world around him. In *8½*'s original screenplay, he even got a bit drunk from the wine – a Dionysiac excitation still manifest in the tremulous glow emanating from the warmed bed, the fresh linen, even a cobweb under the table. Vivid to him, too, are the other *bodies* in the scene: the children naked with him in the bath, the girl who sits above the vat throwing grapes into it, the two nannies who rub him dry, tuck him into bed and kiss him goodnight.

Besides the wine, of course, he is also being bathed in GA's would-be curative nostalgia – with the effect that, to many viewers, this polymorphously sexual atmosphere seems to be nourishing only

healthy buds of normality. The Criterion commentary, for example, unblinkingly observes how 'sweetly' the nannies' kisses are sexualised – as if one of GA's dreams hadn't already shown us a maternal buss going to full mouth! But Fellini, once again his own first critic, has Daumier condemn GA's childhood memories precisely for their 'inoffensive and fundamentally sentimental' framing. We are accordingly invited not only to see this eagerly standardised framing as such, but also to see through it to those perverse elements also recalled and which prove abiding in the man to whom Boy Guido is father.

We notice, to give but one instance, the noticeably good looks and build of the young man who – with a sweetness of his own – dunks Boy Guido up and down in the tub. Fellini was not careless in his placement here; the man's visual assertion anchors the more famous verbal enigma in the episode, likewise suggestive of sexual ambiguity. When the children have been left to themselves, the girl shows Boy Guido a portrait on the wall; its eyes may be made to move by reciting the magic words: 'asa nisi masa'. As we require scholars to tell us, this otherwise incomprehensible phrase is a pig-Latin-like form of 'anima', which is in turn (Fellini being a fresh convert to analytic psychology) Carl Jung's name for the unconscious feminine part of a man's personality.

Without access to this erudition, GA grasps only the insistence of the phrase, not its significance. Sheltered in his unconscious, his enduringly obscure 'anima' animates a whole series of minor –

or minoritised – events in his mental life. Sometimes, it takes the
form of a classically detachable *projection* onto Woman; the harem
is full of women who are all, according to Gloria, who is one of
them, 'creatures of his imagination'. But at other times, more
interestingly, the anima activates an immediate *identification* with
Woman – as when, for example, GA plays distractedly with Carla's
purse. Such identification is broadly on display in the hotel elevator
where – as if belatedly reacting to the joe in the tub – GA finds
himself gazing intently at a handsome young man in the Cardinal's

entourage. More than once, the camera
too lets itself be caught in a similarly
blank-eyed act of man-watching.
It would be a mistake to heat up the
temperature of these fascinated fits into
torrid proofs of a 'gay secret'. On the
contrary, what characterises them is the
coolness, even frigidity, of psychic

foreclosure. They are there and yet they don't seem to matter; they don't seem to matter and yet they are there; in a word, they merely *persist*. (8½, rightly praised for extending the cinematic representation of fantasy and dream, is equally innovative in rendering the no less radical mental state of absent-mindedness.) In the service of sexual normality, these moments constitute no more than a sporadic inefficiency, a kind of ineliminable malingering. 'And yet' – *eppure* – as GA likes to say without finishing the sentence. Reluctance here too.

COMFORT FOOD. Things are much the same with the second memory from a couple of years later, when Boy Guido (Marco Gemini) dances with Saraghina, and is caught and punished by the priests. This memory too courts a sentimental reduction – in the one corner would stand Saraghina, evoking Boy Guido's natural sexual impulse with all the authority of a Willendorf Venus; in the other, the mincing priests, thwarting this impulse with their spinsterish religion of guilt. (If the latter look to us like a 'bunch of old maids', that is because Fellini cast women of a certain age and gauntness to play them.) But to see the memory thus simply is to overlook the monumental visual fact on which it pivots: Saraghina's ass. Saraghina, of course, is a pornographic cartoon of *all* the places where a man may find his pleasure in the female body, and her rumba is carefully filmed so as to rotate them, one by one, into view. But the default framing of her, like a basic dance step to which all variations return, puts her backside at the centre of

obsession. Somehow, the ass is not just one among many sources of
pleasure on her body; it is also the one that masses all the others –
from the 'comparable' breasts to the adjacent apertures of vagina
and anus – in a single but overwhelmingly suggestive clump.

This capacity of Saraghina's ass to picture 'sex itself' has
everything to do with the punishment Boy Guido later receives for
having looked at it. Amid the jeering of fellow pupils, he is sent to 'stand
in the corner' of the classroom; a high dunce cap almost entirely
conceals his eyes, and pinned to his back, so that everyone can read it
but him, a sign says 'Vergogna' (Shame). The scene is modelled on a
famous episode in Dickens, where the young David Copperfield is
humiliated by having to wear a placard on his back. For Fellini as well
as Dickens (whom he adored), the defining affect of character is linked
to this harrowing sense of one's uncontrollable approachability from
behind. The disincarnate author is spared this terror, of course, as are

we, who sit on our behind, and lean against our back, in the assurance that no one in the narrative we are watching or reading will be watching or reading about *us*.[19] But Fellini's visuals make this point psychosexually rawer than it was in Dickens. Boy Guido wrings his hands behind him, as if trying to improvise a fig leaf over what the sign thereby seems to be labelling: his literal ass. Albeit decidedly meagre, and decently covered by his trouser-seat, this ass has become the target of all imaginable public shame. The shots of Boy Guido's contorted hands, each only a second or two long, are similarly incommensurate with the film-long structure of its psychic consequence. The shamed ass, in other words, is of traumatic disproportion. It stands not only behind GA's shamefacedness, but also behind his fear and loathing of collectivity itself. It also seems to determine his fixation on *Saraghina*'s ass, whose insolent grandeur would not precede his punishment, but – projected backwards in time – follow from it, a majestic affirmation of impunity.

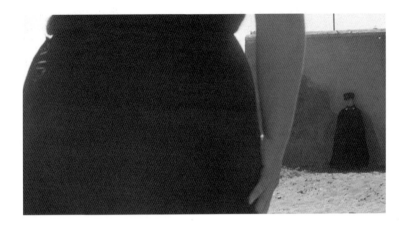

A later, more developed counteraction: Carla has an ass, too, and the first thing GA does on meeting her at the station is put his hand on it: 'How's it doing?'[20] Despite a theoretical wealth of possibilities, Carla's ass inspires GA to but one sexual practice: manipulation. Accordingly, her ass offers him – in the strictest sense – a handful (= Latin *manipulus*), a literal feel for the dreaded social objectification that, by means of this talisman, he may imagine having more than literally in hand. 'How's *it* doing?': Carla's third-person existence is deprived even of personhood, as GA makes himself the agent of a process that, on the receiving end, he has found deeply humiliating. He greets even Rossella in this manner, which seems habitual. Through his becoming an ass man, this man's ass would as good as disappear.

In this sense, the signature Fellini ass is nothing more than the humiliation of the signature Fellini face made palpable to the touch – to the touch, at any rate, of the man doing the goosing. But if GA *does* mean thus to transpose his shame onto women, the manoeuvre is hopelessly ineffective. For Saraghina, Carla and even Luisa never exhibit the least bit of shame around their asses; these are, on the contrary, an obvious source of pride and pleasure to them. In Fellinian Woman, the ass never knows ignominy; it is not merely full

of flesh – it is sure of being. GA's palpations, then, are less likely to be handing off *his* affliction than to be getting in touch with *her* good fortune. (In Italian, *che culo!* means 'what luck!') But how effective is even this manoeuvre? Though the superb female ass may comfort, it must also recall the sorry male ass that, in consequence of its gender, never *can* take such perfect delight in itself. The hands that now – with her pleased assent – casually fondle Carla's ass retain the memory of once writhing defensively in front of his own. (And Carla helps refresh that memory: her secret public signal to GA consists in lowering her hand alongside her ass, turning it backwards and making a gobbling gesture with it.)

More than once, Fellini claimed that his films were part of his personal sexual liberation: 'From first to last, I have struggled to free myself – always from the past, from the education laid upon me as a child.' But though 8½'s satire on GA/FF's repressive Catholic boyhood offers the most direct strategy in that struggle, it also sufficiently indicates why the struggle is doomed, why 'from first to last', it will always require one more effort, destined to fail in turn. In the Fellini ass, desire and shame are linked so intimately, so inextricably, that achieved sexual freedom would be as frustrating as total abstinence.

THIRD COMING. In the sudden euphoria that overcomes GA at the start of the finale, he declares to Luisa: 'How simple it is!' Yet hardly has he spoken these words – vague, but soothingly comprehensive – than he finds to his dismay that 'everything is confused again!' To secure this fugitive simplicity, he is driven to conjure Boy Guido for a third and last time. This final appearance, moreover, is no mere recollection, inhibited by the more-or-less given materials of past record; it is an apotheosis, bounded only by the presumably nonexistent limits of imagination. His school uniform now bleached cherub-white, Boy Guido has come dressed to inspire, not unlike Aquaria before him; and with flute in hand and clown musicians in train, he seems equally prepared to dissolve anxiety in an idyll or to brighten up depression with a circus. For his part, GA speedily confirms the boy in our collective faith in him, laying a hand on his shoulder and whispering marching orders in his ear. The quickie sacrament takes instant effect: the next thing we know, there is GA picking up his megaphone, barking orders through it as if he had never laid it aside. The implication is clear:

with Boy Guido anointed as his assistant, GA is about to direct again, and his block to thaw and resolve itself into the supreme work we have been watching.

At GA's signal, Boy Guido stations himself in front of a curtain, guardian of the revelation behind it. At another signal, the curtain parts, and we see GA's cast and crew descending the tower staircase

en masse. The mood is light, relaxed; people are laughing, chatting, being their 'off' selves. Yet the viewer's joy at this sight may be so acute, and his relief so profound, as to bring him to sobs. For if the 'others' are now indifferent to DA, by the same token they are no longer harassing him; his once petrifying social relations have been made spectacularly easy. In homage to the child who has piped in this vision, GA keeps its elaboration in an ostentatiously childlike register, forming everyone into an elementary circle dance. Thus configured, the social field no longer looks terrifying, and GA readily joins the circle, treading the dance just like the others. Even now he takes the precaution of entering the circle as a married man, with Luisa in tow, as if his social integration might prove difficult without this entitlement, but he no longer objects to being a character, one among many. The imagery recalls the Dance of Death from Ingmar Bergman's *The Seventh Seal* (1957), but only by way of contrast; *8½*'s last and greatest dance is plainly a celebration of Life, a Life whose vital circulation could hardly be more literal – or more literally moving. 'Life is a festival; let's live it together!' It is this pageant of

'simplicity at last', in which the person is whole and the artwork complete – that Boy Guido has been called on to authenticate.

Even as the pageant is forming, however, we may see the signs that it is unsustainable. First, the Cardinal makes a hurried departure, excusing himself from the quasi-pagan circle and so excluding GA from the Church outside of which, the prelate has warned him, 'there is no salvation.' Then, with still less ceremony, Mezzabotta and Gloria (for whom, even now, white will never replace black in point of chic) go their merry way, in another direction. Finally, even those who do enter the ring make a point of reminding us how incorrigibly difficult they intend to remain: GA's mother (Giuditta Rissone) shrugs as witheringly as mother ever did in assessing her son's antics, and Carla pesters him to call her in the morning. 'Yes, yes. Now get in line with the others.' She obliges, though we hardly imagine her staying in line for long. In such ways, this *tour de force* betrays the inorganic forcing essential to it. Small wonder that, insubstantial as a magic trick, it soon vanishes altogether, as abruptly as it came on.

Except for Boy Guido, that is, who remains on hand to attest to the disenchanted state it leaves behind. Still the performer, he continues making vigorous 'directing' motions, but their animation has become compulsive, a reflex of lonely desperation. For night has suddenly fallen over the ring, and even his fellow musicians proceed to abandon him there, as Rota's peppy circus music, bereft of its full orchestration, enters a doleful minor key. We first saw Boy Guido in antisocial flight from the group ritual of the wine bath; in our last view of him – stranded in an empty ring under a glaring spotlight, performing for no one, but as if for life – that early indisposition has developed into total isolation, like a pathogen successful at last in causing illness. And then, so as to spell all this out, the spotlight on him is extinguished and he walks off into darkness. If GA's last gesture was to affirm human fellowship, Boy Guido's is *to leave the ring*, that now-creepy arena of socialisation where he has been deserted by what finally seem, in any case, only the 'imaginary friends' of a solitary child.

'When I am asked if I have children,' Fellini once said, 'I always answer quickly and simply, "No, my films are my children." That way, I finish with the question, and with a subject I never like to talk about.'[21] That way, too, GA's bad answer to the Cardinal's same question – 'Yes ... I mean, no' – may be directly reversed and corrected: 'No ... that is to say, yes!' And inspired by Boy Guido, himself a stand-in for GA/FF's missing child, 8½ is the reparative film-child par excellence; 'film-child' would be the very meaning of its cryptic title, if we take it to refer at once to an opus number, a boy's age and the nearly (but still not quite) complete period of fetal gestation. Yet the film remains massively preoccupied by the subject its director wishes to be done with. Although 8½ joins the long tradition of major Italian films that end on the image of a child, it breaks radically with the affirmative meaning of this image. Here the child is not the avenging angel of the future (*Open City*) or a featureless placeholder for the dialectic on its tortuous but trustworthy way to working-class heaven (*Rocco and His Brothers* [1960]). Nor has he been so suddenly, horribly spoiled by adult reality that his lost value as *tabula rasa* feels, if anything, more precious than ever (*The Bicycle Thief*, *Germany Year Zero* [1948]). He is merely the last avatar of that vast, oceanic sadness to which all the moments of elation in 8½ eventually return, like mania to its mother depression. The harem was sad like a household without children; this child is sad like the child-fantasy of a grown-up with no household. If Boy Guido can't save the director from social unfitness or its attendant melancholy, that is because he shares these things with him as intimately as genes; and if the child can't redeem him, how should the film-child? Watch the end of 8½ and remember if you can that it is a comic film.

THE LOST ENDING. Yet it could have been worse – and apparently was. If the circus finale feels 'tacked on', that is because it *was* tacked on, being literally a trailer that Fellini had never planned as part of the film.[22] For that, as the published screenplay indicates, he

had envisioned a different, darker ending. But once this ending had been filmed, it caused him such uneasiness that, late in editing, he replaced it with the trailer. Then, as if to leave no footprints, he destroyed it. Almost all we know about this lost ending comes from 8½'s published screenplay; Boyer's chronicle of the making of the film; some on-set photographs; and – most evocatively – Mario Sesti's documentary reconstruction, *L'ultima sequenza* (*The Lost Ending*, 2003).

In the lost ending, GA has abandoned his film and leaves the spa with Luisa by train. On board, in the dining car, he finds all the people in his life seated at tables wearing all-white clothes; in their midst, Boy Guido waves his hat at the end of the aisle. It is an epiphany. 'Yes, yes,' GA babbles to the assembly, 'It's right, it's right. I've understood. It's really easy. Yes, everything … is as if … everything together … me … you … oh God, how can I explain it to you? Thank you, thank you, everyone. … All we have to do is not hold back … not object. It's really easy … it's all fine, all fine … provided that …' He takes Luisa's hand, and, like the protagonist of Fellini's earlier *Le notti di Cabiria* (*Nights of Cabiria*, 1957), looks directly at the movie audience. Then, as the screenplay has it, in prose worthy of Zola: 'The screen slowly darkens. From the darkened

screen can be heard only the secure, grandiose, powerful,
unstoppable rhythm of the train, confidently hurling itself into the
night.'

Thematically, there might seem little to choose between the
train ending and the circus ending. Both scenes dress characters in
white for an omnium gatherum and make Boy Guido the lynchpin
of a peaceable vision of life and art.[23] (Even the gesture of taking
Luisa's hand is repeated.) In the aesthetic quality of its images, too,
nothing suggests that the train ending was inferior to its replacement.
Those who saw it remember a 'very beautiful' scene, and the nearest
thing we have to a still from it – a Paul Ronald photograph in Boyer
representing Fellini's shooting view of the car – confirms this. We see
an elegant Orient Express car, widened to appear surreally dilated,
and the whites of clothes, tablecloths, napkins, seat-covers,
lampshades and calla lilies are richly layered against the dark
panelling on walls and ceiling. The set has been lit so that these
predominant whites flatten the image to a dreamlike depthlessness,

and the lacquered wood acquires a crepuscular sheen. The whole bears the unmistakeable stamp of high Fellini.

What is eliminated with the train ending, then, is the only thing it *doesn't* share with the other – namely, the train itself – and the screenplay's overheated last sentence helps us understand why. We know this train. It is the train of nineteenth-century novels, where it is driven by Jacques Lantier over the body of Anna Karenina; the train of golden-age detective stories, where its passengers regularly go missing, or are found dead; the train of early cinema, where it threatens to run down Lumière's spectators; the train of Hollywood genre films, where, if the Western doesn't rob it, the war film blow it up or the horror film fill it with phantoms, the thriller earmarks it for equally unlucky encounters between strangers.[24] Last but not least, it is the train of Fellini's own autobiographical *I vitelloni* (1953), where, as Tatti Sanguinetti has noted, it takes the hero on a journey from which he will never be allowed to return. Yes, we know this train; from the beginning of locomotion, representation has hardly given us another. Freighted with fatality, it clickety-clacks to the very rhythm – 'powerful, unstoppable' – of the death drive.

By all accounts, Fellini's train was eminently worthy of this tradition. Everyone reports being spooked by it. To Tullio Pinelli, one of the screenwriters, it was 'funereal', ghostly; to Anouk Aimée, it was 'mysterious' ('Where were we going? Were we dead?'); and to Lina Wertmüller, then Fellini's assistant director, it frankly 'stank of death'. In the Ronald photograph, it is striking how pointedly the pattern of light and dark reverses that of the opening traffic jam, as if in conclusive response.[25] Then, despite the gloomy congestion in the foreground, there was light at the end of the tunnel; now, it is the foreground that is bright, while the perspective disappears into darkness.

Wertmüller claims that, in rejecting the train ending, Fellini laudably chose the fragrance of life over the stench of death. But he also, more problematically, preferred an extrinsic ending to an intrinsic one. As we've had ample occasion to observe, GA's digressive flights of fantasy all end by landing him back in his starting position with renewed heaviness. If anything, his crisis gets worse over the course of the film, repeating itself in spirals of increasing intensity. This repetition is what the train ending threatens to continue, presumably until GA is totally undone, and his epiphany with him. If there is a problem with this train ending, it is that it suits 8½ all too well. It figures the perpetuation of what has been the film's death-driven logic all along.

It is not surprising that Fellini should finally want to reject this unstoppable locomotive dissipation in favour of the circus ring's holistic binding, even though, as we've seen, the ring is soon overshadowed by melancholy. After all, melancholy might be a psychic price worth paying in order to preserve – as a 'loss' one never gets over – what one would otherwise have lost for good: people, the past, self-ideations. Against the loss of *that* loss, the melancholy that finally enfolds Boy Guido seems to protect him as tightly as swaddling clothes. It is, paradoxically, the guarantee of GA's capacity for memory and fantasy, the two most obvious sources of 8½'s inspiration. Would this child affirm after all? We comprehend why Fellini, usually insouciant in these matters, took such apparent care to destroy the entire footage of the ending: so that it too would be romantically 'lost' to this same all-conquering melancholy. He might as well have burned the photograms one by one, like the letters of a person who has died and is now, by this gesture, about to become immortal.

'No surprise that Fellini should want to reject the death-train,' I just wrote, but in an important sense, rejection did not lie within his power of choice. For 8½ came to have a sort of supplement, or sequel, which resumed the lost ending's fatal voyage. This was 'Il viaggio di G. Mastorna' ('The Voyage of G. Mastorna'), the first project to occupy Fellini intensively after the completion of 8½ and its female double, *Giulietta degli spiriti* (*Juliet of the Spirits*, 1964). Mastorna, played by Mastroianni, was to die in an opening plane crash; and the rest of the film would follow his posthumous existence, an afterlife in which, as if passing through purgatory, he worked through his issues with life and death together.

'Mastorna' may well be the most remarkable movie never made. We recall Kael's objection to the *donnée* of 8½: 'What movie in the half-century history of movies has been held up by the director's having a creative block? No movie with a budget and crew, writers and sets.' But as if to prove his sincerity in delaying the production of 8½ for a few weeks, Fellini held up 'Mastorna' forever. Having spent some of the budget and built one of the sets, he abandoned the project as irrevocably as he abandoned the train ending, or as GA abandoned his entire film in 8½'s original screenplay. An uncongenial producer, the star's other commitments, were minor difficulties; the insuperable one was Fellini's superstitious conviction that the making of the film would entail his own death. He ended up getting sick, and getting out of his contract; so 'Mastorna' became the *other* lost ending to 8½. Fellini later talked of making the film 'someday', even claimed, still later, that it was being made in every film that came after it; it was a thing 'born not to be made, but to permit others to be made'. In short, there was no getting rid of *this* lost ending; Fellini would go on 'losing' it repeatedly for the remainder of his career.

That career would be long – the superstitious aversion to 'Mastorna', or to what 'Mastorna' named, worked like the charm it was hoped to be. But, as in a fairy tale, there was a catch to the charm, a price for such longevity. For the subsequent work disappointed – indeed, fell off so dramatically that 8½, Fellini's greatest film, is also generally considered the last film of his greatness. Not counting the *Giulietta* spin-off, it was the last film that he originated, independent of a literary source or a producer's prodding. It is as if, in giving up – or trying to give up – the obsession with his own death, Fellini had lost some essential component of his creativity.

3 From Substance to Style

LOST IN THE ORIGINAL. While I was writing, in chapter two, on GA's misguided science-fiction project, I consulted the spaceship visit to verify certain 'clinching' details. But no sooner did I begin watching it than these details, vivid in my memory, became diabolically hard to find. In the spaceship's eerie night-world – radiant with balls of light but blurry from their auras, and pervaded with webs of girders and platforms too fine-spun for anyone caught in them to be sure of his whereabouts or destination – in this brave new world where no man was his own, I too had lost my bearings. I had become so distracted by everything I *wasn't* seeking that I half-forgot the original objects of my search – and even when I finally came upon them, almost by accident, they now appeared with all the faintness (and none of the interest) of a palimpsest. To complete the confusion, my disorientation was being literally described in the episode itself, as GA's own: 'I thought I had

something so simple … so simple to say. … Now, my mind is totally confused.' In the end, it was only by adopting a discipline akin to Odysseus's as he passed the Sirens – by resolving to blindfold myself with a fast-forward key – that I could proceed to extract, from this vision more wondrously extraterrestrial than anything in Spielberg, the unassailable evidence for the absurdity, the unworkability, of GA's wretched attempt at science fiction!

The same thing would happen when I re-watched any part of *8½*: the 'thing to say' melted into thin air – or rather, melted into thin air's opposite: the dense, layered atmosphere that was the 'thing to see'. Any argument about *8½*, I soon understood, ran the constant risk of being swamped by an incomparable visual spectacle that, even after the words, meanings, messages had done their work of captioning it, remained fascinating, seductive, ominous – and unknown. This spectacle might be called the film's style. The balls of light in the spaceship episode shone for a purpose that had little to do with illuminating the characters, who were often obscured by their beams, or washed out. Just so, the overall style in *8½*, which might commonsensically be supposed to be expressing GA's condition, seemed to be eclipsing it in the service of a thing, an interest or process, that was, however hard to pin down, undeniably *something else*. Perhaps it was not the person after all that was the ultimate reference of GA's 'nothing', but this style. 'I have nothing to say, but I want to say it anyway': when you came to think of it, could there be a more classic way of affirming a commitment to style – style understood not as a mere failure of 'substance', but as an intentional obstacle to 'substance', always put in its way?

'But in that case, why have you harped on GA's condition, miserable and mediocre, when, by your own admission, the great thing in the film is its style?' – So as to put before us, as brutally as possible, the fact that every great modern style has turned on, not to say turned from: the existential stalemate of its originator. 'And now that you have established this fact, will you finally look at *8½*'s style with eyes wide open?' – Yes – no – I mean, the 'thing to see' is hard to talk about; in that sense, it's hard even to *see*. 'You're being too fine; get going.' – Then let's revert to almost the very beginning, where we left GA in the bathroom, diminished and depressed by his belated incarnation.

THE SPA. As GA's bathroom loses privacy and darkness alike, we pass from the murky enclosures of tunnel and hotel room to the blazing light of the spa grounds and terrace. As a kind of connecting hinge, Wagner's music has been carried over and, with it, many other motifs from the opening sequence. If the people caught in

traffic reminded us of corpses, what is there left to say about the veritable pageant of age and infirmity passing before us now – the men propped up by canes and nurses, the women mummified in hats, veils, nets and dark glasses – except that it is a more literal-minded version of those earlier living

dead? The camera pans through a portrait gallery of people who, even if they weren't wearing 1930s fashions, would look old enough to be GA's parents. Set in a rictus of vivacity, or openly comatose, their faces do not suggest that spring water and mud treatments are likely to regenerate them. Such is the sad company that GA, like just another geezer taking the cure, must now keep; and it confirms him in the deadly condition of a generation whose stories are over.

Carried over, too, is GA's desire for, and desire to escape from, his incarnation. In the first shot of the sequence, GA appears in the unseen, 'missing' form of a figure; people greet or otherwise notice the camera, which we infer must be seeing with his eyes. But no merely ambulant human being could be responsible for the camera angles and movements in the shots that follow. Where, for instance, would GA be standing when, panoramically, we see the entire hemisphere of the spa from above? Or has he, at some unnoticed point in his itinerary, crossed over into godhead? But if he has, then he proves no more able to maintain his divine invisibility than he did among the clouds at the beginning of the film. As if once again brought down from those clouds, he suddenly materialises in the very middle of what we had taken for his own point of view, standing with the other characters in a queue for a glass of spring water.

But the best reason for carrying over the Wagner is that we now witness something genuinely worthy of the elation of a cavalcade. This is the 'ride' the camera takes us on, as – pivoting, dipping, gliding back and forth, up and down over the grounds – it gives us the first comprehensive exhibition of 8½'s famous 'look'. If the first movement of the film initiated the dark drama of a man *who is not man enough*, then this second proposes the dazzling spectacle of a style *that is too much*. In contrast to the hidden personal depths suggested in the earlier movement, this second almost literally wears everything on its sleeve. The first movement merely delivers the agonising, unsatisfactory character-birth of *Fellini*; while the second launches one of the great paradigms of twentieth-century visual culture: what, in the wake of 8½, would be called the *Felliniesque*.

There had been hints, pieces of this paradigm in *La dolce vita* and earlier – hints and pieces that, once it gets named, merit that name. But nothing in Fellini's previous work matches, in thoroughness or insistence, the commitment to style that here becomes nothing less than categorical, an immediate fact that precedes – and perhaps preempts – whatever its images might be thought 'afterward' to say. At 8½'s spa, Fellini becomes what I call a 'stylothete', an artist who poses style as the first principle, the a priori of his work.

GHERARDI, DI VENANZO, FELLINI. For this look, Fellini depends greatly on the collaboration of Piero Gherardi, his art director, and Gianni Di Venanzo, his director of photography. All three artists are aware that they are working at a late moment in the history of black-and-white film, so aware that it might as well be the *last* moment in that history: the moment of self-consciousness, when 'black and white' becomes its own idea. As though to go out in style, Gherardi produces a veritable summa of all that black-and-white film had previously achieved in costume and design. He creates a world that is dressed *for* black and white, by being already dressed *in* black and white. His set and costume design offers more, and denser, black-and-white patterns than – what I take to be his source and precedent here – Busby Berkeley's 'Continental' number from the 1934 Astaire/Rogers musical *The Gay Divorcee*. Di Venanzo has developed an equally vivid technique of black and white, a lighting of high contrasts – and of infinitely subtle nuances within them – that chequers the very atmosphere through which this world is seen. Insolently, he shoots the spa sequence in natural light, that rock on which the Roman Church of neo-realism was founded, and never did natural light look more like photographic lighting, or did the Roman sun throw its rays more 'for effect'. Neither collaborator could be called self-effacing; each is happy to let us see him at the top of his over-the-top game.

But Fellini holds the trump card; and with the virtuosity of his camera, he sweeps up the other two hands into a third degree of

stylisation that is all his own. Gherardi's design, for instance, merely renders the visuals theatrical; it is in the camera's restless 'walking tour' that they become dramatic. Panning this way, that way, Fellini turns this design as one might turn a kaleidoscope whose engrossing patterns, at the very moment they are being observed, have already reformed into new ones.[26]

Observe the complication of black and white that accrues to the parasols alone. First there appears a succession of white parasols; then, for contrast, a cluster of black ones; then, in contrast to the contrast, parasols patterned in black *and* white. The hybridisation ramifies fast and furiously: black dots on white, white dots on black, black-and-white stripes, circular, mitred, with a black dominant, a white dominant, in equal balance. Finally, when GA at last appears on screen and the story may move forward, there collect in his vicinity several black parasols all with white spots, but, as on some infernal eye exam, the spots come in different shapes, sizes and densities. In what the camera's turning and framing have made an increasingly obsessive – and strangely gripping – game of pattern-making, the play of same-but-different seems to reach sheer lunacy. And should we wish to enter this lunacy – to consider whether, among so many dots, there might also be a point – we would hardly have the time; the fascinating patterns will already have passed us by.

To this kaleidoscope, furthermore, pieces of glass are being continually added, so that, with every revolution, its mirrors are absorbing new shapes into its changing compositions. Gherardi's *mise en scène* is fanatically modular, and, as the camera turns, we enter a fantasia of visual rhymes and resizings. Parasol shapes droop into hats, crease into fans, swell into now an *umbrellone*, now, peaked at the top, the roof of an orchestra-stand. Parasol sections, as if scattered from some hallucinogenic bouquet, morph into visors, bandeaux and hat brims; into modernist benches and Deco walls rising above the spring; into the long isosceles triangles that, radiating sunburst fashion from a memorial flower-clock, cause the entire terrace to resemble a gigantic backgammon board. And if we have noticed so many such sections, we may discern still more of them in the arc of our vision itself, as Fellini's pivoting camera serves us one after another 'slice' of life at the spa. Not only is every photogram in the sequence a kaleidoscopic version of every other, the kaleidoscope's very mirroring seems to enter the ever-changing spectacle of what it shows.

Fellini's camera gives a comparable turn to Di Venanzo's photography, dramatising the latter's high contrasts in rapid movements from light into dark, and vice versa. Just when the camera has given us its closest approximation of an establishing shot – an overview of the spa terrace in brutally bright sunlight –

Hat

Fan

Bench

Bandstand

Bandeaux

Visor

Wall

Clock

it suddenly, from within the same shot, dips down to a shaded foreground that we have never seen (and whose whereabouts we will never be able to 'establish'); there two anonymous figures stand with their heads bowed, in apparent imitation of the camera that has just dropped its gaze equally inexplicably. Conversely, in GA's daydream of redemption, the camera spots Aquaria among the shady wood, and fairly floats her across the grounds to serve him a glass of water. If the white dress made her stand out in the woods, the white wall behind the water-trench almost obliterates her in radiance. Di Venanzo's photographic genius for always finding enough shadow to texture an infinity of whites was not quite to the point here. To convey this effect of light sheer and untempered, light 'in itself', Fellini had Enzo Verzini bleach the film in printing it so that, as Verzini puts it, 'I ate up all of la Cardinale except her dark eyes.'

AGAINST INTERPRETATION. Yet why hasn't style stood out in such ostentation before now? After all, the first movement of the film – what I've called the drama of incarnation – can hardly be considered lacking in boldness of shot, set or lighting. But what mitigates the effect of style there is that all the strange images come implicitly framed by an invitation to interpret them. From the outset, a certain symbolic quality has turned each astonishing wonder into an enigmatic sign. The opening of 8½ is a textbook-typical product of 1950s and 60s art-film culture, in which the obscurity of an image inevitably pointed to the profundity of a meaning. In that aesthetic of arcana, everyone must puzzle over what the signs meant; but neither the philistine who found them too deep nor the cinephile intent on getting to the bottom of them ever doubted that they *were* signs, or that they required a formidable degree of 'intellectuality' for their interpretation. What was there on the screen always referred to 'a mental scheme of categories'.[27] The beam of illumination, when it eventually came, might be meagre or uncertain – the kind of wan clarity that caused a film by Bergman, the master of this manner, to be given the English title of *Winter Light* (1962) – but that only better suited the austerity and difficulty of intellectual insight. Accordingly, when Fellini puts light at the end of the tunnel, he is almost hamfistedly reminding us of the symbolic vocation lying in wait for even the strangest images we are watching. And if this isn't enough, he offers a yet stronger guarantee of interpretability:

precisely like Bergman in *Wild Strawberries* (1957), he attributes his
eerie images to a dream, thus authorising us to send it off, with a
perfectly good conscience, to a Freudian – or better, a Jungian –
school where all the wildness will be beaten out of it.

By comparison, the spa shots seem to be doing a lot of nothing,
and doing it as zealously as possible. Arresting, loud, overblown, the
sequence is neither fearful of calling attention to its look, nor
particularly eager to disappear into narrative or symbolic function.
When viewers blithely call the look of *8½* stunning, breathtaking, eye-
popping, a knockout, they name it precisely, for it seems intent on
depriving us, if not of our senses, of our sense. Like the natural light
so unnaturally bright here, this style dazzles rather than shimmers, as
if struck off a surface instead of emanating from the deep. Fellini's
'look' compels *us* to look; but it couldn't care less about making us
see. Brilliant, but not lucid, its images move too fast, teem with too
much odd detail, to be well perceived, let alone pondered or collected
into a whole. They no doubt convey some recurring motifs and even
a general satiric tone, but such minimal efficiency hardly justifies the
enormous effort behind them, or the detail of their delirious
patterning. If they excite intellectual reflection in us at all, it is to
wonder whether intellectual reflection could ever catch so much
'stunning' brightness, could ever render all of it into mere
enlightenment. Of the hermeneutic heaviness that hung memorably
over Alain Resnais' spa in *Last Year at Marienbad* (1961), the air
here is quite free. It is as though, along with GA, *8½* too were seeking
a cure at this spa, and for an identical ailment: the unbearable stress
of manufacturing cultural profundities.

The look of the spa shots is not just indifferent to such
profundities, but positively corrosive of them. As we've earlier noted,
a great deal seems intended in Aquaria's appearance at the spring:
purity, salvation, an ideal of feminine beauty and support. But while
the dress code employed here may be kitschily obvious, its point is
continually being blunted by the visual practice of Fellini's
kaleidoscope. For Aquaria is not the only, or even the most

conspicuous, person in white on the spa grounds. She shares the kaleidoscope with a fat, giggling nun in a white habit; with the haggard, crabby water girls in white uniforms; and even with Daumier, immaculate in a white suit. Given so many valences, the would-be symbolic white can't tell us the difference between the beauty of GA's dream and its utter silliness; between a woman-saviour and a nagging drudge; between creative purity and critical sterility. Wildly overproduced, this white loses the power to mark an antithesis, and so to sponsor the differential process of meaning. Instead, it induces a kind of semiotic fog that confounds opposites that ought to have been as polar as black and white. Even Verzini's bleaching does not make Aquaria a 'whiter' figure than the others, so much as it loses her – along with her upper-case significance – in a thickening of this fog. It eats her up truly, for the resultant confusion of meaning is not all that different, finally, from an erasure of meaning altogether.

'The film becomes a suite of absolutely gratuitous episodes. One wonders what the authors intend.' This is ostensibly a general complaint about GA's film project; but Daumier makes the remark just after the spa shots, which we are invited to take as an example of what he is talking about. His plural – 'the authors' – suggests a cross-reference to the four men credited with 8½'s screenplay: besides Fellini, Pinelli, Ennio Flaiano and Brunello Rondi. But more to our point, it also suggests certain cross-purposes *within* authorship that make 'intention' thus problematic. At the spa, all images seem to have been designed to take priority over their thematic captioning. The captioning hardly ceases for all that, but it never removes this primal luminosity, which baffles any attempt to justify it, apparently even by 'the authors'. Against the aesthetic of deep meaning that governs GA's nightmare, the spa sequence proposes a visual autism.

WORDS AND MUSIC. This visual autism is given an acoustical glaze by Nino Rota's score. 'Between us,' said Fellini of his relation with the composer, 'immediately, a complete, total harmony.' Given the unprecedented unity of music and image in 8½, his immoderate claim has a certain plausibility; a mere still from 8½ will start us humming Rota's music, which, in turn, heard on the radio, will bring the Felliniesque straight to our mind's eye. It is as though each were the necessary complement to the other, the thing required to make it complete. Even when, as for the spa sequence, Rota does not compose the music, but merely chooses it, it remains exquisitely attuned to the complexity of mood, at once grandiose and neurotic, uneasy and triumphant, out of which 8½ develops its defining irony. In the score as a whole, the sheer range of genres at Rota's command – from classical and jazz to pop, Latin and cabaret – seems made to serve the heterogeneity of Fellini's episodic construction; and, within a given track, the composer's subtle modulations of key and tempo effect a perfect match with the director's equally fluid camera movements in the correspondent scene.

Yet Rota's score, for all its near-miraculous aptness, is not the same thing as Fellini's music, any more than Gherardi's set or Di Venanzo's lighting is the same thing as Fellini's camera or editing. Rota's great gifts do not by themselves explain the purpose – lacking in his work for other directors – to which Fellini has subordinated them. 8½'s music, we observe, comes on strong: rarely is there anything understated or subliminal about these instrumental bursts that arrive suddenly, at full volume, and in a form of a set piece; they summon us to attention as sharply as does the orchestra at a musical when a 'number' is about to begin. Sometimes, in fact, this music literally *does* herald a number: the women's dances, the spa nightclub act, Boy Guido's band of clowns. And even when this is not the case, their aggressive musical accompaniment makes scenes *feel* like numbers; the mud baths, the press conference, the finale – set to Rota's music, these elaborately choreographed pageants become weirdly reminiscent of the hoedowns of *Oklahoma!* (1943) or the rumbles in *West Side Story* (1961). Despite their inferior quality, the two musicalisations of 8½ – Bob Fosse's broad cinematic *hommage* in *All That Jazz* (1979) and Maury Yeston and Arthur Kopit's more faithful Broadway adaptation in *Nine* (1982) – show a dead-on understanding of the film's implicit tendency.

As is well known, Fellini filmed much of 8½ with music blaring on the set. Although Rota had yet to write the score, scenes were performed and shot to loud, vehement music. Even in being produced, in other words, the image was thus musically prepossessed against the words being spoken in it – words that, in any case, were often gibberish, to be dubbed in with sense later. Rota's eventual score perfects this lamination of the image, so that when the word comes – to caption, to interpret – it never seems to come *from* the image. Fellini's famously slipshod post-synching abets this alienation of the word, which arrives from what is literally an audible distance, secondary, belated, expungible.[28] (In English-speaking countries, the old borderless white subtitles produced a congenial effect: words were stamped on an image that, itself often saturated by white, made them almost illegible.) We have remarked that the most important words in the film are 'I have nothing to say'; let us now further remark that they are spoken by GA off screen! Conversely, the bravura sequences in 8½, all flooded with music, are also either wordless or (what comes to the same) cacophonous, audible only as the white noise that, in any case, the music will have already drowned out. Through music, 8½ tenders the vacuum-packed purity of a silenced cinema.

LES DEUX CÔTÉS. The last shot of the first movement's drama of incarnation ends with the image of a director: GA, shrinking lower and lower into depression. The first shot of the second movement's spectacle of style also ends with the image of a director: the orchestra leader, upright and even uplifted by low-angle framing. This conductor's face is as nondescript as a face ever gets in Fellini; and its unremarkable quality goes hand in glove with its absorption in the music and the work of making music. Fellini's diptych of directors is emblematic of the two directions – the 'two ways', as Proust would put it – that the film initially posits for its visual practice. In one direction lies the man, marked out by his fearful shortage of being and meaning; in the other lies style, which never acknowledges, unless it be to destroy, any order besides its own to which it is required to be sufficient. In the

man, substance is inchoate, inadequate to the desired form; it is a drag on everything. In style, substance loses any such power of pressure, dissolving into a play of movement and light; marks of dishonour, feelings of shame, behaviours of abashment – these suddenly have no more pertinence than the rules of a schoolmarm in the Wild West, or the laws of a nation in a foreign embassy.

In complaining about Fellini's self-indulgence in 8½, critics have never known how to distinguish personal from stylistic abandon; for them, the film-maker who would speak of himself is no different from the style that has nothing to say. Such critics have a point: a thin line separates the bad form of flaunting the self's injured condition – and so of reminding us of the social order's brutality – from the bad form of flaunting style's *uninjured* condition – and so of implying that something exists outside this order, some capacity or force on which it hasn't put the mark of its vicious discipline. This, however, is not the point that 8½ makes in its opening premises. For here, decidedly, style *isn't* the man. The man is a character without 'character', whereas style is personality without 'person'. The character refuses style's wealth of textures; style in turn refuses the confinement of human being to a unit of socialisation, a situation of answerability. These are the poles that 8½ establishes for itself; they are its 'black and white', the binary that shapes every episode that follows. At first separate, they enter into intimacy as GA sets about addressing the psychic and artistic business before him. In the process, they prove to be the basis for the social engagement that 8½ is not widely supposed to have.

THE CARDINAL. In demonstration of this last claim, I turn to an episode that, as the most marked instance of the film's 'two ways', offers an object lesson in the relation between them. This is GA's visit to the Cardinal. But 'visit' and 'episode' are inevitably misleading terms for an encounter that – in defiance of the Cardinal's spareness – 8½ represents twice.[29] The first meeting takes place on the spa terrace, where the Cardinal is seated and Guido brought to join him;

it consists almost wholly of the brutal social catechism that I have already quoted in full. The second occurs during the mud treatments; GA has been taken to the anteroom of the Cardinal's *cabina privata* and the two converse through a connecting window. The Cardinal still does most of the talking and again says precious little: 'Man was not born to be happy. Outside the Church there is no salvation. Whoever is not of the City of God belongs to the City of the Devil.' But 'first' and 'second' aren't quite the words here, either. GA's assistant has set up a single meeting, and each of these two meetings is treated like the only one; the earlier conversation does not promise a subsequent encounter, nor does the later one acknowledge a previous one. 'You have five minutes,' the Cardinal's own assistant tells GA in the anteroom; but in saying this, he *holds up ten fingers*. The discrepancy suggests that these five minutes remain from an original ten – that there are not two meetings, but two halves, or dimensions, of what we're to take as a single visit. Fellini is offering us a narrative hendiadys: two episodes for one.

On the terrace, GA and the Cardinal are filmed with cinema's most conventional (hence, most natural-seeming) means for representing dialogue: alternating shots of each speaker mixed in with two-shots of both together. But even this routine cinematic embodiment involves GA in as much discomfort as would a police interrogation. As we've seen, the Cardinal's questions aren't all that far from one, and there is a last little touch to crown them. As a bird is heard singing overhead, his eminence remarks that it sounds like a sob. GA can hardly miss the allegory – no blue bird of happiness, no nesting brood for *him* – and while the prelatic entourage throw edified eyes to heaven, he casts his own downward, as though, in his shame and confusion, he wanted to disappear.

In the 'second' meeting, that is just what he does. We see him, by way of preparing for it, already covering his body in the generic abstraction of a suit; and by the time the camera accompanies him into the anteroom, this body has vanished altogether and won't reappear until the next sequence. Though the scene at first uses the connecting window to suggest GA's point of view, no human figure stationed at the window, even equipped with a very flexible neck, could see the images we do. More than once, the camera films the Cardinal from behind the very sheet meant to cover him from GA's sight. And in dramatic contrast to the conventionally filmed first meeting, the second abounds in proofs of the Felliniesque. Whereas the first took place in a grove, whose natural green hues are hard to forget even in a black-and-white film, the second matches its black-and-white film stock to black-and-white objects: white cloth, black cloth, white tile, black mud. As in the spa sequence, gratuitous, but insistent patterns come to mesmerise our attention. The two men who first put the sheet in place are dressed in white; the two men who later remove it are habited in black; and of the two men who, in

between times, wrap it around the Cardinal, one wears white and the other black. Shades of those sunshades! Once again, GA/FF rescinds his incarnation, even as, in somewhat spiteful exchange, the Cardinal's scrawny body acquires added emphasis. Once again, he replaces a socially stigmatised self with a spectacular affirmation of sensuous, but senseless visuality.

Yet, as dramatised in this hendiadys, the escapism is too obvious to accomplish real escape. In any event, when the visit is over, GA's disappearance is followed by a reappearance on which his story and character-state are resumed. This game of peek-a-boo – played all through 8½ – ensures that style never stands free of the stylothete's personal back-story for long. The demonstration ought to chime well with the prevailing intellectual mistrust of style as an evasion of hard social facts. Instead, however, critics have repeatedly turned the film's own point against it – 'the sheer beauty of Fellini's film is deceiving us'

(John Francis Lane)[30] – as if GA/FF were simply wearing camouflage rather than complexly pointing it out. What's said to be wrong with *8½*'s style invariably amounts to some version of GA/FF's failure, as Eric Rhode put it in 1963, 'to confront his social obligations'.[31]

The observation is at once perfectly true and completely wrong-headed, and it is both things for the same reason: GA/FF has himself pleaded guilty to the charge. On the one hand, his admission that he *is* avoiding his social obligations is too lightly made to persuade us that he has a proper recognition of their importance. To draw a metaphor from his religion, this is a *bad confession*; the penitent has told his sin without true contrition. On the other hand, however, the self-declared irresponsibility of Fellini's style announces not a lapse to be deplored, but an intention to be understood. For every 'strong' style – I mean one, like Fellini's, of blatantly insufficient substance – marks a refusal to come to terms with a world whose social organisation it lets us perceive, in specific ways, as intolerable. More: every such style mounts a positive offensive against this organisation, an offensive that, if we choose to understand it, makes the familiar unmasking of style as 'denial' look like a kind of denial itself. Our reflex demystification of Fellini's style has kept us from reflecting on this style as the agent of a demystification of its own; and if this style rather too obligingly invites us to denounce it in the name of social truth, it also, more interestingly, exposes a certain basic lie in this truth.

In the second meeting, for example, the Cardinal says little more than 'Outside the Church there is no salvation.' The doctrine is as narrow as its expression is concise. (It was, in fact, the motto of Origen, the early-Church philosopher who carried ascetic economy to the point of self-castration.) Yet the Cardinal says the phrase over and over, in Latin and Italian variations, with an intonation that recalls GA's own earlier singsong, relieved of self-irony. The restrictive doctrine gets thus enhanced by the hypnotic pleasure of repeating it, a pleasure that the doctrine cannot even acknowledge, much less explain. What the Cardinal 'has to say' cannot account for his very saying of it, which so falls 'outside the Church'.

Likewise, in the scene as a whole, the Cardinal's ascetic seclusion proves strangely dependent on the aesthetic atmospherics of his stagy 'private compartment' with its full complement of costumed attendants. To be sure, there is a Roman Catholic gloss on everything in the room: the glass blocks sift light like a cathedral window; the porcelain tiles display cruciform patterns; and the pedestalled basin vaporises the spring that GA's doctor had earlier called 'holy water'. As for the Cardinal himself, steam clouds around him like incense, while assistants flank him in the manner of acolytes – his very sheet drapes him in a nonce chasuble. Yet clearly he is not officiating at high mass; nor is his secretary, who ritualistically kneads the mud in the foreground, preparing for a sacrament. Whereas in Church liturgy, each gesture holds a precise significance, the formalities observed in the Cardinal's bath serve no purpose beyond the elaboration of a spectacle that seems all the more unwarranted for taking place in the private compartment of a man who insists on his austerity. Though everything in the scene connotes the Catholic rite, nothing denotes it; the rite is present not in its truth, but only in its spectacular, sensuous fascination.[32] Albeit stark naked, then, the Cardinal is unconsciously bathing in *a style without substance*. In the last analysis, he is simply a GA who doesn't own up to it. He too is an ungenitor, his only children being (as he would doubtless claim) his flock. He too doesn't say enough to cover – rationalise and so conceal – his pleasure in 'saying it anyway'. But, unlike GA, the

Cardinal doesn't acknowledge any of this. He can hardly afford to:
his unknowing is not just the privilege, but also the precondition of
his entitlement – which now, on Fellini's showing, seems more unfair
than ever. Simply for closeting his style, we are asked to resent this
man as fully as if, in some more orthodox satire on the Church, he
were parading his catamite.[33]

BROTHER DAUMIER. We are probably not greatly troubled by the
fraud at the heart of the Cardinal's austerity; the Church is no
authority that mystifies *us*. But the insight gets more edge if we shift
the site of its demonstration from the Cardinal to Daumier, 8½'s
other abstinent anti-hero. The demonstration itself is quite similar.
This critic's doctrine: 'True perfection is in nothingness.' His values:
the 'truly necessary' and not a bit more. His models: Mallarmé's
eulogium on the blank page and Rimbaud's renunciation of writing.
'We're stifled,' he pronounces, 'by words, images, sounds, that have
no right to exist.' And he carries this half-ethical, half-aesthetic
doctrine of strict justification into his social persona as well, fearing
that his presence is not 'indispensable', or that his notes may not be
'much use'. He wears an exactingly white suit, and from time to time
his hand must brush off the dust that has defiled it. Yet here too, Attic
starkness dissimulates, almost literally, rococo underwear. The bleak
day suit gives no hint of the florid pyjama-and-dressing-gown
ensemble that serves as its wearer's dishabille. No more does

Daumier's austere creed account for his glib volubility in professing it when GA's film is being scrapped. If anyone were ever pleased by the sound of his own voice, it would surely be this popinjay as he sings – and sings – his ongoing aria in praise of silence. And whatever fervour he can't release in lilting cadences (more singsong) escapes through gesticulating hands, as they embroider 'the truly necessary' with additional *fioriture*. (It is no accident that, in the background of one of his harangues, we hear an opera singer embellishing a Chopin nocturne.) With so much self-voguing, Daumier's performance exceeds, and so contradicts, his claim to represent intellectual essence; like the Cardinal's, it shows more than can ever be said in it. If only under our $8\frac{1}{2}$-trained eyes, this implacable superego of the 'something to say' reveals himself as a monster of more style than substance – differing only in scale and in daring from the one he castigates, named GA.[34]

THESIS. Fellini's camera uncovers such hideaways of style everywhere it looks, like an ultraviolet light inducing fluorescence. Herein lies the slyness of $8\frac{1}{2}$'s own style, its odd, fine power of critical observation. As we've just seen, this style is particularly hard on the severe. The ascetic person, the dogmatic utterance, the authoritarian order – these are the targets that it likes to show harbouring secret flamboyance. Recall that, among the pupils jeering at Boy Guido in his dunce cap, many accompanied him to Saraghina's bunker, but simply didn't get caught; their hyperactive taunting at once screened and sustained their own sexual excitement. *8½* brings out a similar logic of disavowal around style. In every quarter where stylistic surplus is categorically refused or condemned, there we are sure to find its unacknowledged production and enjoyment. Invariably, renunciation or censure proves hysterical, accompanied by a theatrics whose own excesses furtively indulge the 'tendencies' being rebuked. Every fakir has a glass display case.

But the hypocrisy of Daumier and the Cardinal only spotlights the bad faith at the core of every character's social being in *8½*. On the one hand, the Fellini character is always performing who he 'is', soliciting his socially recognised identity with endless histrionics, as if to say, 'See? I really *am being* whom you must therefore take me to be.' On the other hand, the same character typically stops short of acknowledging the performance *as* one, lest he suggest that such identity is not stable, natural, whole or fully internalised. Recall Sartre's pronouncement on style in writing: 'To be sure, style makes the value of the prose, but it should pass unnoticed.'[35] *Mutatis mutandis*, this is the logic of the social presentation of self in *8½*. Style finds its social use-value only in being sublimated; if we are obliged to notice it, we must wave it away like second-hand smoke, but provided we don't notice it, it is our sociability's very breath.

MISTRESS CARLA. If there is any character in *8½* with an 'avowed' style, it is the vain, vulgar, silly, superficial, pea-brained, pleasure-loving Carla. With her abundance of outfits and ass, her perfect indifference to 'position' intellectual and social, this material girl embodies the Felliniesque vision better than anyone. Yet with no mind or thoughts to put in it, as inane as the characters in the comic books she reads, she is less of a person than anyone, too. Her lack of an inner life means both that she can know no shame and also that no one can take her seriously. Her style makes her, socially speaking, *deniable*. 'If there's anything I find insulting,' GA cries to Luisa, 'it's the notion that people could think I would go around with a woman

who wears a get-up like that! You've seen how she dresses, haven't you?' But we have seen GA apply make-up to Carla himself; and he obviously takes as much pleasure in her *Vogue* knockoff (which in fantasy he has even Luisa admiring) as in her piggy sexuality. In 8½'s world, Carla is the designated style-scapegoat: the 'tasteless' public depository of the others' secret appetites.

We first meet her descending from a train; and GA prudently hides her in the Albergo della Ferrovia, a shabby pensione so close to the station that you can hear the train whistles in the dining room. As the film's personification of its style, Carla is thus linked to what was going to be the film's image for death. Even as the film stands, this picture of vitality is the only person in a whole spaful of *curistes* to get sick; while everyone else merely complains of mentalistic 'headaches', Carla burns deliriously with fever, even babbling out last

bequests. Here too, of course, 8½ remains a comic film, sparing us the Victorian outcome it parodies. It is nonetheless suggestive that Carla gets sick from the same Happy Water that everyone else is drinking for health. For unlike the others, content with their prescribed dose, Carla has guzzled. And so where style is concerned, too: she seems to represent to everyone the state of having 'too much of a good thing' – and so perhaps to reconcile everyone to the state of never having enough of it. If Carla channels the power of style to *wear out* the person (erode it, turn it inside out), she also trivialises this power by allowing us to imagine it confined to her entirely trivial self; that is what scapegoats do for us. Precisely as the personification of Fellini's style, therefore, she represents it falsely. She limits the antisocial force of visual autism to a ghetto, where, as the exception, it is resubmitted to social rule.

ART ISN'T EASY. Style 'unchained' is more than a negative social value; it is the value of social negation itself. That is why it cannot be practised in *8½*'s social world without being either hypocritically denied (the Cardinal, Daumier), or homeopathically marginalised (Carla). Fellini's style is so profoundly antisocial that it doesn't let us envision revolution or even social change. It offers only the practice of irrelevance, sustained with – and even like – a vengeance. Far from arguing or apologising for this irrelevance, his style simply puts it before our eyes. Its only 'reason' is the self-evident pleasure we take in it: the pleasure of annihilating a social relation felt to pertain to us so thoroughly that, like GA in traffic, we are in danger of suffocating. While we watch *8½*, such mere pleasure proves as compelling as the harshest social necessity.

But style, in this sense, is also a rare thing. Most styles are simply not powerful enough to achieve social negation even momentarily. And if they are, they tend either to dialecticise it as the ruse of redemption after all, or to trivialise it as so much detailing on a winsome niche brand. The latter course, we know, was embraced by Fellini's own style after *8½*. It turned itself into Mistress Carla, glibly self-contained in tics-become-trademarks. 'That's Fellini for you!' became the all-sufficient explanation of Fellini's strangeness, which, thus canned for safe consumption, proved less and less strange. As if anticipating the depleted post-modern 'citations' of *8½* – most recently by Todd Haynes in *I'm Not There* (2007) – Fellini's subsequent style devolved into an otiose footnote to what it had been. This dulling of style-as-negation has broader causes (cultural, commercial) than the merely existential fear of death that Fellini evinced in abandoning *8½*'s original ending and the 'Mastorna' project; but it joins with that fear, as its formal counterpart, in determining the artistic downturn of his career. With the exception of *Toby Dammit* (1967) – Fellini's great, nauseated self-parody – *8½*, the first great instance of his style, is the last time it contains wholly live cultures.

Finale

SYNCOPATED CLOCK. Almost as prominent on GA's person as his wedding ring is the watch fob attached to his left jacket lapel. It is equally remarkable that the watch itself remains unseen; GA never withdraws it from the pocket where it presumably but unprovably lies. The tease culminates at the press conference where, as GA leans over a mirrored table, the fob chain is shown leading only back to

itself, not unlike a figure eight, or the letters in *otto*. Precisely in being occulted, this old-fashioned pocket watch contrasts with the modern self-winding wristwatch ostentatiously conferred on GA by Pace. As the gift of his producer, the wristwatch inevitably signifies the time of production – a reminder to GA (which Pace later makes explicit) that 'the film has got to begin and begin now!' But what manner of time would the pocket watch be keeping?

It is too weirdly presented – or rather, absented – to be a simple internalisation of Pace's admonishment. On the contrary, even unseen, it clicks at all points with GA/FF's manifold reluctance to heed this admonishment. It is at once the *futile* watch never consulted, or perhaps, like its owner, not doing its work; the *personal* watch keeping its private, individualist time in defiance of

mundane time-clocks; the *auteur's* watch never showing a face;
the *surrealist* watch suitable for clocking dreams and daydreams; the
artisanal watch requiring manual care; the *irregular* watch that, even
with such care, may run fast, or slow, or just stop, inescapably tied to
deviance; and finally, the *obsolescent* watch, itself out of style, given
to men who (with one exception) are retiring from the work force.

To whichever such symbolic valences we may attach it, it is an untimely timepiece, irrelevant to the socially recognised or 'standard' time being told in the world around it.

Carried in GA's left pocket, moreover, the watch lies opposite the gun that gets pointedly hidden in his *right* pocket and is the instrument of his suicide. The watch would not only be differentiated from the time of deadlines; it would also be distinguished from the moment of death, which the deadlines have been helping to hasten. ('Under the gun' has its Italian equivalent: *con un fucile puntato*.) If the gun is what kills GA, the watch, lying over his heart like a mysterious pacemaker, would be what makes him tick. Signifier of life, then? Only if we overlook its more ominous connotation as the *railway* watch, worn by the train conductor (the exception noted above) on the job. Signifier of death, in that case, idly biding its time before eventual service on the death-train? Perhaps, but as 8½ stands,

GA never boards that train; and even if he did, it is doubtful that this watch, with its film-long association with errancy, could have provided an objective correlative for the train's 'secure ... unstoppable' rhythm.[36] If the watch's material concealment points to an intimate time in *8½*, its uncertain symbolic location makes the meaning of that intimacy ambiguous. 'Time in *8½*' indeed! – would the title be, after all, a musical signature?

O MY MASTER BUILDER! By way of this enigmatic watch, I offer a last observation about style in *8½*, regarding, precisely, the question of its tempo. For all Fellini's reputation as a maestro, his style is too restless to project the authority or assurance of a master. Consider the 'absolute style' of Hitchcock or Ozu (or for that matter, Jane Austen or Flaubert): a style whose total control and constant poise suggest that its author everywhere occupies the place of an omniscient, perfectionist demiurge. A film is being made, a book is being written, in what seems, while we watch or read it, the only conceivable way it can be done. In these cases, style is an inalienable possession of the author's that, once found, is never lost; nor is anything else mislaid in a creation where every word or image has its proper place, and time runs to a palpably measured cadence, like a train on schedule. God may be often presumed dead in the story, but he proves doubtlessly resurrected in the style; here, there *is* a special providence in the fall of a sparrow, not to mention in every cross-fade and cutaway. Their very perfection, one might say, suits the works of absolute style only too well. They may speak *of* a world without transcendence, they might even, in certain respects, speak *for* it, but they hardly seem affected *by* it, inasmuch as their style tends to supply us the very experience of wholeness and consistency that is felt to be missing from the world under depiction. This enchanting state of exemption is what we commonly understand by the term masterpiece.

In Fellini, style never possesses this even, constant quality. Here, the camera does not sit tranquil on Ozu's tatami, or sally forth with the dignity of Hitchcock's dolly, but rushes about to a frankly nervous rhythm; and when it cuts to a detail, it seems not to be pointing, or even observing, so much as making (wild, empty, 'mere') gestures in the commotion. Unlike Hitchcock's tracking shots, Fellini's have no obvious journey's end – a key, a man who twitches – to give their movement a point; even when they end by surprising us, as with the sudden dip into shadow in the spa sequence, the surprise is inconsequential, an accent on the overall distractedness. What's more, this flurry of activity subsides as abruptly as it began, not because it has achieved a climax or catharsis, but for no better reason than that it appears to have simply run down. Whereas absolute style strikes us as both a *total* fact and one essentially accomplished *before* the work (in storyboards or equivalent predeterminations), Fellini's style manifests itself in short, disconnected spasms of vivacity that seem to belong only to the moment of their urgent execution. In charge of this execution, then, would not be a master, for whom even the future is always already past, but a virtuoso, for whom time is nothing but the swiftly passing present.

Partial, sporadic, limited to a 'piece', 'passage' or 'moment', virtuosity never commands the whole in which it appears only as a discrete, contrastive episode. Virtuosity is essentially hurried, even short-lived: so many notes, so few measures: that difficulty is the gauge of its necessarily quick and belaboured brilliance. (Rota's greatest contribution to 8½ is to score, and so underscore, its virtuosic style.) No doubt, virtuosity is style's assertiveness, its way of conscripting our attention and diverting it from so-called matters of substance. But what also gets asserted in the process is style's evanescence. For a while, of course, it seems as if time itself cannot fly faster than the nimble fingers dancing over the keys, but before long, as everyone knows and expects, the virtuoso performance unwinds, like a pocket watch, until it finally – and often quite dramatically – just stops. Virtuosity is style's *memento mori*, addressed to all (the stylothete included) who would make style their supreme being. Here, the negative force of style is not simply directed to the social world or to the 'things to say' there; it is also finally turned on style itself. Virtuosity breaks style into 'pieces', shrinks it to the fitful and fleeting, a mere tremulous mirage that, having come into view, is already going away. Undermining the absoluteness of style, and hence its capacity for consolation, Fellini's virtuosity bespeaks perhaps his most caustic espousal of the modern condition: even this god lies dying in the general twilight.

THE END OF THE MASTERPIECE. The best as well as most famous example of this virtuosity remains the finale. Although, as I remarked earlier, the train ending was more suitable to the film's *thematic* structure, the finale far better serves its *stylistic* project. Indeed, the finale's virtuosity may be shown to offer a more radical negativity than the death-train, one that inheres not simply in a represented object, but – more intimately – in the film's own texture and rhythm. We recall that, while Daumier is inveighing against images 'that have no right to exist', GA conjures up gratuitous apparitions of Aquaria, Boy Guido, Saraghina, the Cardinal and others, all in shining white raiment. If we earlier complained that we couldn't tell Aquaria's 'good' white from the 'bad' white of her run-down fellow attendants, that indifferentiation has now become the very point of GA's visionary exercise: the ubiquity of white clothes augurs total spiritual unification.[37] With even the Cardinal numbered among the apparitions, one can hardly avoid thinking of what, in his favourite theologian Origen, is called *apocatastasis*: the restoration of all created spirits, including devils and the damned, to their original loving oneness with God.[38] From the man 'who doesn't love anybody', as Claudia puts it, GA seems about to turn into a quasi-divine medium of universal love.

When a curtain is set up amid these transfigured figures, we expect their intimations to yield a full-scale revelation. But though the curtain parts with a great flourish, what it discloses is a mass spectacle of people *dressed as they always were*. Only just begun, Fellini's White Party is already over: the universal blanching will not take place. (And to make the point still clearer, the Cardinal reappears in the next shot, now wearing a black hat and a distinctly unbleached, presumably scarlet cloak.) Despite the magician helping with the proceedings, the trick seems only meant to show that there is nothing inside the hat that we haven't already seen. Is this failure – aesthetic and not just spiritual – responsible for the tearful, jubilant release the moment makes us feel? It announces, in any case, the most important stylistic difference between the finale and the original train ending. There, of course, every character *was* dressed in white, and all were arranged in the stringent perspective of the dining car. GA's universal acceptance coincided with a total stylisation that was the expressive collateral for the implied transcendence-in-death.

By contrast, the finale stages the very abandonment of this idea, which is started, then proven to have no traction. What is surely the most misremembered detail in all *8½* – that everyone is wearing white at the end – is only a mirage that the film, having called it up, spectacularly dissipates.

The similarly all-encompassing idea of the circle dance that replaces it will be abruptly abandoned as well. GA and Luisa seem the last to join this dance, but no sooner have they done so than it is shown from a viewpoint outside its circumference; demonstrably incomplete, it too then disappears, another mirage. (Before it vanishes, it exhibits the classic sign of virtuosity: *it accelerates*.[39]) And so the erratic finale keeps changing course, discarding every temporarily ruling idea; the white clothes, the circle dance, the clown band, Boy Guido – each is sampled, then quickly broken off in favour of the next 'piece'. The only thing that might seem total is the darkness concluding the series – but even this is not held for half a second before, with a change of music, credits come on screen to lighten it up.

The finale of *8½*, then, is really a string of finales, each at once *coup de théâtre* and anticlimax, in the hectic manner of fireworks. All through this whirligig, the vital and the moribund, stylistic abandon and the abandonment of style, continually give way to one another. Iconic, uniform and deathly, the beautifully consistent train ending was meant to lay the finishing, finalising touch on a masterpiece. Iconoclastic, miscellaneous, violently 'alive', the finale is meant to *flaw* this masterpiece, by dramatically attacking, again and again, the total style that is its premise. As we've seen, 8½ first laid down that premise in the exhaustively designed spa sequence, and part of what gives the finale its essential delicacy, despite its big effects, is that it draws back from that earlier drop-dead elegance. It is Fellini's retraction: a last exhibit, this time *within* the domain of style, of that mix of hesitancy and resistance, that vexed pause for thought, which we have called his reluctance.

We have seen this reluctance determining Fellini's narrative embodiment, but all along it has been determining his stylistic practice, too. Recall that GA's on-and-off character presence was matched to an oppositely phased intermittency of style, which would wax as he waned, and vice versa; the same alternation that kept character from definition deprived style of continuity. Now, in the finale, as style submits to the anticoagulant violence of virtuosity, its discontinuity becomes more spectacular than ever before. Yet the spectacle can hardly be confused with that abject surrender of stylistic excess to sober substance, which is often promoted as the ultimate sign of artistic and personal 'maturity'. On the contrary, it lays the foundation for an aesthetic politics refractory to that maturity. For if the finale keeps refusing to let style gel, it does so only to sabotage style's self-betrayal in the form of the masterpiece, that 'enduring', even 'timeless' work where, by dint of 'discipline', 'restraint' and 'work', everything hangs together and nothing is out of place. In the last analysis, the masterpiece's supreme coherence would offer only an aestheticisation of social fatality, an imaginary order that lets every real order dream of being similarly inalterable. By spoiling this coherence, virtuosity remains truer to style's antisocial impetus than the making of artistic masterpieces that is, after all, style's most honourable social end.

HIGH TIME. *8½* famously blends together the remembered past, the experienced present and the fantasised future. Even today, these temporalities are somewhat confusing to distinguish at first; they all seem so equally *present*, so equally in relief. Every cinematic image, of course, manifests itself in the now of its on-screen projection, but *8½*'s present tense has been particularly remarked for its unrelaxed tension. It inaugurates that generally distinctive time-image in Fellini which, with apt ambiguity, Gilles Deleuze has called 'a parade of presents that pass' – that in passing by are becoming past. In this race to self-abolition, 'they run not to the future, but to the tomb.'[40] Never more so than at its most thrilling, Fellini's parade of presents beats out what may still be called, in this graver sense, the time of our life. 'High time': our English phrase for impatience does equally well for Fellini's hyper-present: a moment at once perfectly ripe (high summer, high noon) and already *beginning to go bad*.

Thus the high time of *8½*'s virtuosity amplifies the anxious heartbeat of its middle-aged hero, to whom Rossella's spirits say straight out, 'You don't have much time.' Thus it heightens the manic-depressive drama contained in his every perception, memory and fantasy. (Would style, then, at last become the man? Yes, but only insofar as the man has now been subsumed under style's own pulse.)

The virtue of virtuosity is not to abolish his crisis, or to make him feel better about it; it is to intensify the crisis in the near-musical clarity of formal abstraction. This virtuosity is no more able to hide anything 'behind' it than to hide itself; in that respect, it may even be said to reveal. Its mirage lets us know – more sharply than mere water deprivation ever can – the unbearable magnitude of our thirst.

Acknowledgments

TITOLI DI CODA. Nothing makes me feel more like an auteur than rolling off the names of what auteur criticism would have called my *équipe*: the familiars on whom I depend, again and again, for ideas, treatments, editing, research and above all – for an auteur stands in need of this no less than a person – continuity. Let me first thank, then, those I do not thank for the first time: Lee Edelman, Philip Fisher and Laura Mullen; Adam Feldman, Catherine Gallagher, Amanpal Garcha, Neil Hertz, David Kurnick, Joseph Litvak, Kent Puckett, Hilary Schor, Garrett Stewart and Alex Woloch. This circle has happily widened here to the indispensable collaboration of Frank Burke and Rob White; Jessica Brent, Candida D'Aprile, Chris Jensen, Robert Noble, Ben Parker, Lance Rhodes, Mario Sesti and Joshua Weiner. At the Centro Sperimentale di Cinematografia in Rome, Giuseppe Rotunno graciously shared his recollections of Fellini's 'Mastorna', and the library staff offered kind and copious assistance. I am indebted to David Secchiaroli for permission to reprint his father Tazio's photographs, and to the Rockefeller Foundation for a month's residency at the Villa Serbelloni on Lake Como, which quite rivaled the spa in *8½* as 'a beautiful place to work'. And under the vague but essential heading of Morale, I thankfully acknowledge Robert Beck, Oscar Bucher, Susan Chen, Jason Erikson, Stephen Friedman, Thomas Hostetter, Ken Kishimoto, Jane Little, Ida Miller, Richard Peña, Elizabeth Simpson, J. D. Stanga, David Tavernas, Clara Tuite and Rebecca Walkowitz. This essay is rather naturally dedicated to Franco Moretti; he's been with me since my first film.

Notes

Bibliographical note

The version of 8½ used here is the Criterion Collection DVD; this transfer was made from Mediaset's 35mm Fine-Grain Master Positive, which was duped from the original 35mm camera negative.

In Italian alone, the Fellini bibliography could make up a small volume; indeed, thanks to the commendable efforts of the library at the Centro Sperimentale di Cinematografia in Rome, it already is one. For my English-speaking readership, I mention three pioneering works that remain basic operating equipment. Deena Boyer's on-set account of the making of the film, *The Two Hundred Days of 8½* (New York: Macmillan, 1964), will never have a rival for the kind of information it offers. Nor have we yet fully harvested the abundant crop of formal observations contained in Ted Perry's early *Filmguide to 8½* (Bloomington: Indiana University Press, 1975). And Charles Affron's *8½* (New Brunswick, NJ; Rutgers University Press, 1987) provides the only accurate continuity script existing in any language. With occasional modification, my quotations from the film have been taken from this script. Of recent Fellini scholarship, the best comprehensive studies are Tullio Kezich, *Federico Fellini: His Life and Work* (2002), trans. Minna Proctor (New York: Faber and Faber, 2006) and Frank Burke, *Fellini's Films: From Postwar to Postmodern* (New York: Twayne Publishers, 1996). Curiously, Fellini has tempted few critics to match him in formal innovativeness; I except

Sam Rohdie's *Fellini Lexicon* (London: BFI, 2002), whose imaginative organisation unsettles the Fellini we thought we knew.

1 A recent anthology of contemporary perspectives on Fellini pointedly omits it from 'the films that best demonstrate Fellini's continuing relevance as an arbiter of social value' (Frank Burke, Preface to *Federico Fellini: Contemporary Perspectives*, ed. Frank Burke and Marguerite R. Waller [Toronto: University of Toronto Press, 2002], p. viii).
2 This point was first theorised in Christian Metz, 'Mirror Construction in Fellini's 8½', *Film Language: A Semiotics of the Cinema*, trans. Michael Taylor (Oxford and New York: Oxford University Press, 1974), pp. 228–34. In Metz's original French, the term rendered as 'mirror construction' is *construction-en-abyme*, a heraldic term designating a coat of arms on which is pictured a second, smaller coat of arms just like it. More important, the term recalls André Gide, who first used it metaphorically to evoke the novel-within-a-novel structure he developed in *Paludes* (*Swamplands*) and *Les Faux-Monnayeurs* (*The Counterfeiters*). As Metz duly notes, Gide's work is a major precedent for 8½. Just as *Paludes* 'is about a novelist writing *Paludes*', so '8½ is the film of 8½ being made; *the film in the film is … the film itself*' (p. 232).
3 The usual explanation for the title, originating with Fellini, is that '8½' represents an opus number. Before 8½, Fellini had made six films and three film segments (counted as 'halves') for a

total of 7½; 8½ would be, then, his eighth-and-a-half film. See Boyer, p. 7. It has also been suggested that 8½ might be the age of Boy Guido in the 'asa nisi masa' episode or the age of Fellini's first remembered masturbation. But all these explanations are extrinsic to the film's own evidence, and their positivism (or, in Fellini's case, pretend-positivism) does away with what is most striking in the title and therefore most in need of being explained: its absurdism.

But even looked at thus schematically, '8½' betrays a certain redundancy, a kind of needless excess. Making the same point already carried in the '8', the '½' spoils the neatness of both the point and the figure. No less than the pesky pennies on a balance sheet, or the unwieldy fractions in stock prices, it inspires a wish to *round it off*. Not by chance does the first number on screen after the title happen to be 99, the line-number of a bus caught in the traffic jam; and not by chance is it followed later in the film by

My own understanding of the title, therefore, hinges on the fact that, in the film itself, '8½' *has no referent whatsoever.* It does not function as a number, designating a specific quantity (of years, of films), but only – and only in the title – as the *image* of a number; it is as such that we are invited to study its shape and logic. I have claimed that the '8' figures an ambiguity between one and two, an ambiguity that becomes literal in the '½'.

the double 8s on some posters. In Fellini's little jokes, the wish is fulfilled, but overeagerly: 99, for instance, rounds off 8½ not once, but twice, producing a tautology of its own, not to mention a number that inclines us to round it off in turn. The excess of the '½', it is implied, will recur in every attempt to eliminate it.

4 As we will come back to these two reviews, here are the relevant excerpts:

I think that 8½ is the worst film ever made by a major Italian film director. It is a disgusting piece of self-exhibitionism; it wallows in self-indulgence and self-abuse. Its pretentiousness is totally gagging; it is witless and senseless, a public indiscretion. (Joseph Bennett, 'Italian Film: Failure and Emergence', *The Kenyon Review* [Autumn 1964], p. 739)

Some years ago a handsome, narcissistic actor who was entertaining me with stories about his love affairs with various ladies and gentlemen, concluded by smiling seductively as he announced, 'Sometimes I have so many ideas I don't know which one to choose.' I recall thinking – as I edged him to the door – that he had a strange notion of what an idea was. … [The director hero of 8½] is like the movies' famous couturier who can't decide what he's going to do for the spring collection ('I've simply got to get an idea. I'll go mad if I don't. Everybody's depending on me'). (Pauline Kael, *I Lost It at the Movies* [New York: Little, Brown, 1965], p. 261)

5 Fellini used the same helicopter to film GA ascending. *La dolce vita* is written into the scene in another way too: the underpass itself is located at the end of the Via Veneto, where the street joins the Villa Borghese – on the precise route of the number 99 autobus we see amid the gridlock – and it seems to have been built after *La dolce vita*, during the rash of modernisation before Rome's 1960 Olympic Games. It is as though, in Fellini's imaginary, the underpass were a literal first answer to the question: where does he go from *La dolce vita*?
6 This brevity, of course, is abolished in a still, where we have all the time in the world to find Mastroianni handsomer than ever.

7 Peter Bogdanovich, *This Is Orson Welles*, revised edition (New York: Da Capo Press, 1998), p. 138.
8 As the fingers grasping through the grille at the end of *The Third Man* are Carol Reed's. See also Tom Gunning on Fritz Lang's hands as an emblem of film authorship in *The Films of Fritz Lang: Allegories of Vision and Modernity* (London: BFI, 2000).
9 For the origin of the name 'Guido', we must go back to the end of *I vitteloni* (1953), where Moraldo has boarded a train that will take him away from provinciality forever; he waves farewell to a boy named Guido, whom he seems to take as a figure for the youth he is leaving behind. 'Addio, Guido' is his last line in the film, but it is spoken not by the actor playing Moraldo (Franco Interlenghi), but by Fellini himself. 'Guido', then, already points to Fellini's artistic distance from himself.
10 Fellini once said of Antonioni: 'He is an artist who knows what he wants to say'; he is, in other words, as unlike GA as possible. Within hours after *L'avventura* was booed at Cannes, its author retained the presence of mind to draft and issue a rigorous defence of the film. And even when, in *La notte*, he does represent a creative crisis, his novelist hero (also played by Mastroianni) experiences it as almost the exact reverse of GA's: 'I know what to write, but not how to write it.'
11 Costanzo Costantini reports that, after Fellini's Oscar for *Amarcord* (1973), he called the maestro to request an interview:

'But what do you want me to say? I truly don't know what to say?' …
'All I want is five minutes, maybe ten.'

'Well, come to the Via Sistina tomorrow morning, but I tell you again I have nothing to say.'

Just before nine I was at his office.

'I'm sorry you've come all the way here for nothing,' he said to me shaking my hand and embracing me.

There followed a brief silence; then he added, 'I really don't know what to say to you.'

There followed another brief silence; then he lay down listlessly on the sofa and gestured to me to take a chair beside him.

He talked nonstop until one-thirty. (Costanzo Costantini, *Conversations with Fellini*, trans. Sohrab Sorooshian [New York: Harcourt Brace, 1995], p. viii)

12 Thus, to take just one among many examples, the question 'Do you really think that your life can be of interest to others?' predicts its later echo in *Time* magazine: 'Fellini … has a singular personal problem … but unless Fellini's problem has been preying on the mind of the viewer, he may not care to take on the director's doubts and confusions. … Says Fellini, "[Making the film] was a liberating experience." But is that a reason for showing it publicly?' (*Time*, 28 June 1963, p. 82). I will have more to say about this phenomenon in note 32.
13 Didier Eribon, *Insult and the Making of the Gay Self*, trans. Michael Lucey (Durham, NC and London: Duke University Press, 2004), p. 61.
14 In this, she differs radically from Fellini's wife, Giulietta Masina, who of course acted in many of his films, which were themselves created around her personality. Luisa's braininess (her glasses) and star presence (her clique) exist only as the unrealised potential of a housewife, often shrewish at that.

Fellini makes this change, I think, to clear the marriage bond of compatibility, thus rendering the bond itself more abstract, unmotivated by anything except social necessity.
15 The moment refers to Fellini's own child with Giulietta Masina, who, born sickly, died after a week. It also, I think, tropes on this dialogue between the police commissioner and the American wife in De Sica's *Stazione Termini* (1953):

COMMISSIONER: Do you have children?
WIFE (who has been caught embracing a
    man not her husband): No, I mean, yes.

16 This figure had already appeared in *La dolce vita*, where Marcello refuses to start a family with Emma, and Steiner murders his own children.
17 Federico Fellini, *I'm a Born Liar: A Fellini Lexicon*, ed. and trans. Damian Pettigrew (New York: Abrams, 2003), p. 96.
18 Or, for that matter, as the naively high-minded drama that Leopoldo, the wannabe playwright, is writing in *I vitelloni*; here too the pure women are habilimented in white.
19 See also D. A. Miller, *The Novel and the Police* (Berkeley and Los Angeles: University of California Press, 1988), pp. 211ff.
20 In this endowment, she is decidedly unlike Luisa, whose physical refinement – along with GA's sexual indifference to it – owes a lot to her seeming not to have an ass. Poor Luisa! Everyone admires the physical elegance that is inseparable from her slender form, but no one physically desires it. (Even Enrico [Mark Herron], the puppy-man in her entourage, can't get himself beyond merely doting.) And poor Anouk

Aimée! Famously, Fellini put freckles on her face and black-framed glasses over her eyes, but it is not this uglification – in any case, unsuccessful – that makes her an untouchable here; it is her very beauty: distinguished, spiritual, carnally minimalist. In Claude Lelouch's *A Man and a Woman* (1966), this same beauty will qualify her to play the essence of femininity, but in 8½ refinement is not voluptuous, and she must stalk the film, literally fuming from the everlasting cigarette in her mouth, with the angry exasperation of a rich person stranded in a country where her money is no good. The words of the French actress played by Madeleine LeBeau would sit even

throughout the film, he simply went through Aimée's own closet. If her innate good taste could be trusted to do his work, it did not inspire him to do much of it himself.

But to this rule of respectful indifference there comes a thrilling exception when Luisa finds herself, for the first time in over a year, dancing with GA; he declares himself refreshed by her smell, her lightness, and even teasingly asks her if Enrico isn't 'a little bit in love' with her. Then, with a sly look lit up with pleasure, she breaks out of his arms and struts into a jaunty solo swing that, for sheer ecstasy, has nothing to envy Gloria's twist or

better in this French actress's mouth: 'Don't tell me that I'm beautiful. The way you say it sounds like an insult!' Here, even the homosexuals are disappointing: Piero Gherardi laboured mightily on Carla's *redingote*, the extravagantly vulgar outfit that is one of his most memorable creations; but for the elegant white tunic that Luisa wears

Saraghina's rumba. A violinist instinctively leaves the orchestra for her side, knowing that this performance deserves a personal accompaniment. For a brief moment, everyone, even on screen, becomes a rapt spectator of Luisa's 'turn', her transformation into the charismatic star who plays her. Perhaps as a concession to her newly enthusiastic admirers, she sways newly discernible hips.

In Paris once, at the Brasserie Lipp, the author had the privilege of dining across the room from Anouk Aimée, who looked – as is no doubt common on such sightings – more beautiful in person than she had ever been on screen. His giddy thought: perhaps she would be out of cigarettes, would accept one from his own stock. '– Ecco la sigaretta. – Grazie.'

21 Charlotte Chandler, *I, Fellini* (New York: Random House, 1995), p. 44.

22 In making his subsequent film, *Giulietta degli spiriti*, Fellini repeated the stratagem, this time without backsliding. He let Italian television show a purported vignette from the film before its release; but the teaser was nowhere to be found in the finished film ('Playboy Interview: Federico Fellini', *Playboy*, February 1966, p. 55).

23 It has not been acknowledged how extensively both endings are modelled on the last volume of Proust's *Recherche*. The 'sudden joy' that makes GA 'tremble' in the present ending is plainly meant to resound with the equally unexpected 'joy' that overwhelms Marcel 'like a certainty' in the courtyard of the Guermantes mansion. And both endings to 8½ make us understand the degree to which the film has been analogising its entire structure to that of the *Recherche*, a work whose subject is finally revealed as the struggle to reach the threshold at which the work becomes possible. Fellini, of course, was fond of boasting that he had never read Proust (or Joyce *et al.*). It is safe to assume, however, that, among his fellow screenwriters, the novelist Ennio Flaiano was not so unlearned. In

any case, as Fellini also liked to say, one doesn't have to have read a writer so profoundly influential as Proust to have absorbed his lesson, particularly in this schematic form.

24 The only celebration comes in the musical (*The Harvey Girls*), *par excellence* the genre of denial.

25 Woody Allen seems to have understood this. The beginning of *Stardust Memories* imitates 8½'s traffic jam, but the site of the hero's panic has been changed from a car to a train carriage.

26 I take this metaphor from Fellini himself. In the 1960 letter to Brunello Rondi that first outlined the idea for 8½, he evoked the film as 'a magic kaleidoscope' (Affron, p. 234).

27 Susan Sontag, 'Against Interpretation' (1964) in *Against Interpretation* (New York: Farrar, Strauss and Giroux, 1966), p. 10. Ultimately, Fellini anticipates Sontag's impatience with intellectualist interpretation, but Sontag may well have the opening sequence of 8½ in her sights when she writes: 'Like the fumes of the automobile and of heavy industry which befoul the urban atmosphere, the infusion of interpretations of art poisons our sensibilities' (p. 7).

28 As early as the film's premiere in Rome (12 February 1963), there were complaints about 'a dubbed sound track that seems to run on a completely different plane from the image' (*The Times*, 13 February 1963, p. 13).

29 In the letter to Rondi, Fellini envisioned a worldly yet mystical bishop who would stand for the Church in which his hero was raised. 'He should be a character who awakens memories, guilt complexes, and all kinds of other messes' (Affron, p. 232). Fellini also imagined a conversation between this prelate and his protagonist, though having no idea 'what they would have to say to one another'. In the actual film, the bishop has been raised to the cardinalate and, as part of his elevation, he loses the flashy mitre and crosier that, as leftovers of the original

30 John Francis Lane, 'A Case of Artistic Inflation,' *Sight and Sound* (Summer 1963), p. 135.
31 Eric Rhode, review of 8½, *Sight and Sound* (Autumn 1963), p. 193.
32 Earlier, GA had used just these terms to evoke the Cardinal that he was planning to put in 'I, Guido': 'A prince of the Church seems to [the hero] the

conception, still adorn the woman, a countess, who auditions for the part in Guido's screen tests. The few quirks he possessed in the letter – asthmatic cigarettes, insomnia, a Mercedes – have also been eliminated and, by the time we first see him, silently sharing the hotel elevator with GA, he evinces utmost clerical sobriety. It is as if, to be an effective reminder of GA's psychic 'messes', he had himself to be tidy in the extreme – or as if his character were meant to represent the Church not just as an outmoded, pathogenic creed, but also as this rather more appealing possibility of psychic minimalism.

guardian of a truth that he can no longer accept, although it still fascinates him.'
33 The sex angle is not altogether lacking: the Cardinal is worldly enough to crack a gay joke at table. But just as Fellini eliminated the Mercedes, so he made the joke unintelligible to anyone who wasn't already familiar with it. For those not in the know, I tell it in full: A youth in confession: Father, I had sex with Mario.' The priest: 'What – with a communist?!' The Cardinal explains for the slow-witted: 'He didn't say "a man" – get it?'
34 In 8½'s early critical reception, this irony, easy to grasp, proved

impossible to take. It encountered resistance – a veritable circling of the wagons – from the entire critical establishment, regardless of how its members felt about the film. Even the ones who liked the film, though they might sharply disagree with Daumier's specific objections, retained intact the overall critical attitude that he embodies – and that Fellini deconstructs. Despite the portrait's provocation, not one of these admirers paused even a moment in assuming their professionally given entitlement to objectivity and distance; and their allegiance to the 'something to say' remained as unshaken as their belief in the transparency of their means to say it. It is further striking that – unlike the many engaging polemics against the film – the panegyrics on it rarely interest us in their own right as critical writing. Curiously stolid performances, they seem to be unconsciously taking every precaution not to get caught up in the innovative, sometimes even called liberating processes they are celebrating. 'Here is a piece of entertainment that will really make you sit up straight and think'; yes, but you couldn't say the same of that sentence, written by Bosley Crowther in the *New York Times* (6 June 1963, p. 36). The early praise for 8½ was universally insincere in just this way, a flattery without imitation.

The early censure was insincere for opposite reasons. Critics who did *not* like 8½ had so little obstacle put in the way of their identification with Daumier that, with total unawareness, they repeated his exact charges, often word for word. Here, for instance, is Daumier on GA's portrayal of the Church: 'If you

really want to engage in a polemic around Catholic consciousness in Italy … well, my friend … in this case, believe me, what you would need above all is a higher degree of culture.' And here, in his review of 8½ for *Rinascita* (the Communist Party weekly) is Mino Argentieri on Fellini's portrait of 'a Catholic in crisis': 'What, at bottom, one notices in 8½ is the lack of culture, which becomes unforgivable in proportion to the ambitions harboured by the auteur' (*Rinascita*, 16 February 1963, p. 24).

Of the many cases of this self-oblivious plagiarism, the most impressive is John Francis Lane, who, having played a hostile critic at the press conference *in* the film, went on to write a negative review *of* the film for *Sight and Sound*. Though the review accuses Fellini of 'artistic inflation', its treacherous bitchiness confirms the exactitude of at least one of the film's caricatures.

Such intense mimicry of Daumier causes hostile critics to reproduce not only his argument, but his hypocrisy as well. Their strictures, like his, are always animated by an unacknowledged but effective exuberance that begs to be called Felliniesque. Though Kael, in her personal anecdote, makes a point of 'edging' the obnoxious bisexual actor out the door, we can hardly forget that it was she who brought him in, and who has just now brought him on, as she will the hysterical couturier, for our entertainment; she's made her review a freak-show of the very kind she deplores in Fellini. And what can Joseph Bennett have in mind in mouthing off about how 'gagging' the film is, except a wish to throw up in front of us, like a diner in *Satyricon* (1969) before the fact? In similar self-ignorance, most reviews 'against' 8½ channel both the narcissistically indulged self and the ostentatious, unjustified style that they consider the film's egregious failings. In a word, they become Daumier by refusing to understand Fellini's portrait of him.

35 Jean-Paul Sartre, *What Is Literature?* [1948], trans. Bernard Frechtman (London: Methuen, 1950), p. 15.

36 By contrast, in the 1930s Italy Fellini remembers in *I clowns* (*The Clowns*, 1971), the railway watch is carried by the station-master, whom we see bring it out with a flourish, inspect it, compare its time to the station clock's and at last give the signal for a waiting train to depart. Yet even this spectacle of fascist accuracy falls victim to Fellinian 'confusion': the train seems to leave on time, but the station-master, displeased by the passengers' insolence to him in passing, somehow arranges for it to leave a second time, now under the intimidating observation of a fascist official. What time is it this time?

37 Only a year or so after 8½, this beguiling idea furnished the basis of what remains a popular attraction at Disneyland: 'It's a Small World'.

38 'Apocatastasis', *The HarperCollins Encyclopedia of Catholicism* (London: HarperCollins, 1995).

39 This acceleration is taken further at the end of *I clowns*, where a clown's funeral procession is held in a circus ring. As a voice (Fellini's?) keeps shouting 'Faster! Faster!', the old clowns in the cortège pick up the pace until they are almost sprinting around the ring. One sprains his ankle, and several, exhibiting symptoms of oncoming heart attack, drop out from exhaustion.

40 Gilles Deleuze, *Cinema 2: The Time-Image*, trans. Hugh Tomlinson (Minneapolis: University of Minnesota Press, 1989), p. 91. Deleuze's elaboration of the Fellinian present (pp. 88–93) is well worth consulting in full.

Credits

8½ di Federico Fellini
Italy/France 1962

Created and Directed by
Federico Fellini
Produced by
Angelo Rizzoli
Story
Federico Fellini
Ennio Flaiano
Screenplay
Federico Fellini
Tullio Pinelli
Ennio Flaiano
Brunello Rondi
Director of Photography
Gianni Di Venanzo
Editor
Leo Catozzo
**Art Director and
Costumes**
Piero Gherardi
Music
Nino Rota

Production Companies
Angelo Rizzoli presents
a Cineriz production
uncredited
Francinex (Paris)

Production Supervisor
Clemente Fracassi
Production Manager
Nello Meniconi
Unit Manager
Mario Basili
Production Secretaries
Albino Morandin
Angelo Iacono

2nd Unit Director
Alessandro Von
Normann
Artistic Collaborator
Brunello Rondi
Assistant Director
Guidarino Guidi
Assistants [Directors]
Giulio Paradisi
Francesco Aluigi
Continuity
Mirella Gamacchio
Camera Operator
Pasquale De Santis
Assistant [Editor]
Adriana Olasio
Assistant Art Director
Luciano Ricceri
Set Dresser
Vito Anzalone
Costume Assistant
Orietta Nasalli Rocca
Wardrobe Mistress
Clara Poggi
Make-up
Otello Fava
Hairstylist
Renata Magnanti
**Technician
[Colour Grader]**
Enzo Verzini
Negatives
Dupont
Prints and Processing
Istituto Nazionale Luce
Music Publisher
CAM
Sound
Mario Faraoni
Alberto Bartolomei

uncredited
3rd Assistant Director
Lina Wertmüller
Still Photographers
Tazio Secchiaroli
Paul Ronald
Costumes
Leonor Fini
Hairdressers
Eugenia
Filippo
Script Translator
Eugene Walter

CAST
<with>
Marcello Mastroianni
Guido Anselmi,
the director
Claudia Cardinale
Claudia, the star-actress
Anouk Aimée
Luisa, Guido's wife
Sandra Milo
Carla, Guido's mistress
Rossella Falk
Rossella, Luisa's friend
Barbara Steele
Gloria Morin,
Mezzabotta's fiancée
Madeleine LeBeau
French actress always
asking about her part
Caterina Boratto
unknown older beauty at
hotel and in harem
Edra Gale
Saraghina

Guido Alberti
Pace, the producer
Mario Conocchia
Conocchia, production
manager
Bruno Agostini
Agostini, 2nd production
secretary
Cesarino Miceli Picardi
Cesarino, 1st production
secretary
Jean Rougeul
Daumier, a writer
Mario Pisu
Mario Mezzabotta,
Guido's old friend
Yvonne Casadei
Jacqueline Bonbon, aging
soubrette in harem
Ian Dallas
Maurice,
the magician
Mino Doro
Claudia's agent,
'Super Tarzan'
Nadine Sanders
flight attendant from
Copenhagen
Georgia Simmons
Guido's grandmother
Hedy Vessel
Hedy, harem woman
with many costume
changes
Tito Masini
The Cardinal
Anne Gorassini
Pace's girlfriend

Rossella Como
Tilde, Luisa and
Rossella's friend
Mark Herron
Enrico, Luisa's timid
admirer
Marisa Colomber
nanny in black
Neil Robinson
French actress's agent
Elisabetta Catalano
Luisa's sister
Eugene Walter
American journalist
Hazel Rogers
young black dancer in
harem
Gilda Dahlberg
American journalist's
wife, writes for 'ladies'
magazines'
Mario Tarchetti
Claudia's press agent
Mary Indovino
Maya, mind-reader who
works with Maurice
Frazier Rippy
the Cardinal's lay
secretary
Francesco Rigamonti
a friend of Luisa's
Giulio Paradisi c.s.c.
friend
Marco Gemini
Boy Guido at school

<and with>
Giuditta Rissone
Guido's mother
Annibale Ninchi
Guido's father

uncredited
John Karlsen
face in traffic jam; priest
in hat fetching Boy Guido
from Saraghina
Roberto Nicolosi
Guido's doctor
Alfredo De La Feld
member of the Cardinal's
retinue
Sebastiano Di Leandro
member of the Cardinal's
retinue
John Stacy
the production
accountant
Alberto Conocchia
production manager
Riccardo Guglielmi
Boy Guido at farmhouse
Roberta Valli
older little girl at
farmhouse
Palma Mangini
old peasant woman at
farmhouse
Eva Gioia
Eva, young girl in
Cesarino's bed
Dina De Santis
Dina, young girl in
Cesarino's bed
Maria Tedeschi
priest who heads Guido's
school
Luciana Sanseverino
patient taking waters at
the spa
Luciano Bonanni
fakir Siva announcer

Olimpia Cavalli
Signorina Olympia,
screen-test Carla
**Maria Antonietta
Beluzzi**
screen-test Saraghina
Matilda Calnan
a friend of Luisa's; an old
journalist
Ferdinando Guillaume
[aka **Polidor**]
clown in the parade
Maria Raimondi
nanny in black
Grazia Frasnelli
seamstress in production
office
Gideon Bachmann
journalist at press
conference
Deena Boyer
journalist at press
conference
Elizabetta Cini
screen-test Cardinal

Sonia Genser
screen-test Luisa
Alan Helms
journalist at press
conference
John Francis Lane
journalist at press
conference
Maria Wertmüller
mannish woman at spa

**Black and
White**/1.85:1/Mono

Released in Italy by
Cineriz on 15 February
1963. Running time:
114 minutes.
Released in France as
Huit et demi by Columbia
on 29 May 1963. Running
time: 114 minutes.
Released in the US by
Embassy Pictures on

25 June 1963. Running
time: 135 minutes.
Released in the UK by
Gala Film Distributors
Ltd on 22 August 1963.
Running time:
138 minutes 4 seconds
(BBFC certificate A).

Filmed from 9 May to
14 October 1962 at
Titanus [Titanus–Appia]
Studios (Rome, Italy) and
on location in the
Cecchignola military
reservation in Rome, and
in Tivoli, Filacciano,
Viterbo and the beaches
between Ostia Ostia and
Fiumicino (Italy).

Credits compiled by
Julian Grainger

List of Illustrations

While considerable effort has been made to identify the copyright holders this has
not been possible in all cases. We apologise for any apparent negligence and any
omissions or corrections brought to our attention will be remedied in future editions.

8½, Cineriz di Angelo Rizzoli/Francinex; p. 2 – on-set photograph by Tazio Secchiaroli,
© Tazio Secchiaroli/David Secchiaroli; p. 11 – M. C. Escher's 'Moebius Strip II', © 2008
The M.C. Escher Company, Holland. All rights reserved. <www.mcescher.com>;
Soviet poster of 8 ½, author's collection; p. 24 – *Divorce Italian Style*, Galatea Film/Lux
Film/Vides Cinematografica; pp. 25 and 42 – on-set photograph by Tazio Secchiaroli,
© Tazio Secchiaroli/David Secchiaroli; p. 64 (bottom) – *The Seventh Seal*, Svensk
Filmindustri; pp. 67 and 69 – *L'ultima sequenza*, Sciarlò; p. 68 – on-set photograph by
Paul Ronald; in Deena Boyer (see Bibliographical Note); p. 78 – *The Gay Divorcee*, RKO
Radio Pictures.